The everyday world at your fingertips

PICTURE DICTIONARY
PORTUGUESE

www.berlitzpublishing.com

Distribution

UK, Ireland and Europe:
Apa Publications (UK) Ltd;
sales@insightguides.com

United States and Canada:
Ingram Publisher Services;
ips@ ingramcontent.com

Australia and New Zealand:
Woodslane; info@ woodslane.com.au

Southeast Asia:
Apa Publications (SN) Pte;
singaporeoffice@insightguides.com

Worldwide: Apa Publications (UK) Ltd;
sales@insightguides.com

Special Sales, Content Licensing and CoPublishing

Insight Guides can be purchased in bulk
quantities at discounted prices. We can
create special editions, personalised
jackets and corporate imprints tailored to
your needs. sales@insightguides.com;
www.insightguides.biz

First Edition 2019

Contact us

Every effort has been made to provide
accurate information in this publication,
but changes are inevitable. The publisher
cannot be responsible for any resulting
loss, inconvenience or injury. We would
appreciate it if readers would call our
attention to any errors or outdated
information. We also welcome your
suggestions; please contact us at: berlitz@
apaguide.co.uk

Berlitz Trademark Reg. U.S. Patent Office
and other countries. Marca Registrada.
Used under licence from the Berlitz
Investment Corporation

Series Editor: Carine Tracanelli
Editor: Urszula Krajewska
Head of Production: Rebeka Davies

Series design: Krzysztof Kop
Picture research & DTP design:
bookidea
English text: Carine Tracanelli &
Barbara Marchwica
Translation & simplified phonetics:
Aligua
Photo credits: all Shutterstock and
Fotolia

Introduction

Whether you are a total beginner or already have a sound knowledge of your chosen language, this Berlitz picture dictionary will help you to communicate quickly and easily. Packed with 2,000 useful terms, it covers all everyday situations, whether you're applying for a job, going shopping or just getting around. See, understand, memorise: visual learning by combining a word with an image helps you remember it more effectively as images affect us more than text alone.

To get the most out of your picture dictionary you can search for words in two ways: by theme (women's clothes, sporting facilities, hobbies, etc.) or by consulting the index at the end. You'll also find important phrases surrounding a topic in each chapter, ensuring that you have the foundations you need for communicating.

Each word is followed by its phonetic transcription to make sure you pronounce each word or sentence correctly. You will find a helpful guide to pronunciation in your chosen language on pages 7–10.

Note that the terms in this picture dictionary are always given in their singular form unless they are generally only used in their plural form. All nouns ending with o, u, i or consonants are masculine. All nouns ending with a, e or ão are feminine. All exceptions from these rules are marked up with *m* for masculine or *f* for feminine. Genders are provided in both the translation and phonetic transcription, ensuring you can communicate in all variants.

Berlitz are renowned for the quality and expertise of their language products. Discover the full range at www.berlitzpublishing.com.

Table of Contents

Pronunciation

This section is designed to make you familiar with the sounds of Portuguese, using our simplified phonetic transcription. You'll find the pronunciation of the Portuguese letters and sounds explained below, together with their "imitated" equivalents. This system is used throughout the picture dictionary; simply read the pronunciation as if it were English, noting any special rules below.

Stress has been indicated in the phonetic pronunciation by capital letters. If a word ends with m, s or a vowel the penultimate syllable is stressed, e.g.: **fazem** (FAH-zain), **sabes** (SAH-bsh), **escola** (sh-KOH-lah). If a word ends with a consonant other than m or s, the last syllable is stressed, e.g.: **amor** (ah-MOHR), **capaz** (kah-PASH). The rules above are not applied when a word has an accent mark. The acute accent ´ indicates stress, e.g. **sábado** (SAH-bah-dooh), **sósia** (SAW-ziah).

There are some differences in vocabulary and pronunciation between the Portuguese spoken in Portugal and that in Brazil or African countries – European Portuguese speakers easily understand Brazilian Portuguese speakers; not so much the other way around. This picture dictionary uses the Portuguese spoken in Portugal.

Consonants

Letter(s)	Approximate Pronunciation	Symbol	Example	Pronunciation
c	1. Before e and i like s in *see*	s	**centro**	SEHN-trooh
	2. Otherwise like k in *kit*	k	**carro**	KAH-rrooh
ç	Like s in *simple*	ç	**aço**	AH-sooh
ch	Like sh in *shovel*	sh	**chave**	SHAH-v
g	1. Before e and i like g in *gentle*, but softer	j	**girafa**	jeeh-RAH-fah
	2. Otherwise like g in *guitar*	gh	**garfo**	GHAR-fooh
h	Always silent		**harpa**	ARH-pah
j	Like g in *gentle*, but softer	j	**loja**	LOH-jah
l	Like l in *lemon*	l	**lado**	LAH-dooh
lh	Like lli in *billion*	ll	**colher**	kooh-LLIER
nh	Like ni in *onion*	ni	**sonhar**	sooh-NIARH
r	1. Trilled when at the beginning of the word, like a hard h	rr	**rio**	rreeooh
	2. When anywhere else in the word like r in *road*, but softer	r	**criança**	kri-AHN-sah
rr	Trilled when at the beginning of the word, like a hard h	rr	**carro**	KAH-rrooh

The letters b, d, f, l, m, n, p, q, s, t, v and z are pronounced approximately as in English

Vowels

Letter(s)	Approximate Pronunciation	Symbol	Example	Pronunciation
a	1. When at the end of the word like a in *apron* but softer	ah	casa	KAH-zah
	2. Otherwise like a in *father*	ah	carro	KAH-rrooh
ã / â	Like an in *ant*	an	artesã	arh-TEH-zan
à / á	Like a in *father*	ah	carro	KAH-rrooh
e	1. When it stands alone or at the beginning of the word like e in *English*	ee	elefante	e-leh-FAN-t
	2. Like e in *happen*	e	feliz	f-LISH
	3. Like e in *elevator*	eh	metro	MEH-trooh
é	Like e in *elevator*	eh	metro	MEH-trooh
ê / en	Like e in *scent*	en	doente	dooh-ENT
i	Like i in *wind*	i	guia	GHI-eh
o	1. When it stands alone or in the end of the word like oo in *roof*	u	banco	BAN-kooh
	2. Otherwise like o in *oil*	o	sol	SOL
ó	Like aw in *awful*	aw	pó	PAW
õ	Like o in *loin*	oin	botões	booh-TOINSH
u	1. Like oo in *roof*	u	puro	POOH-rooh
	2. In some cases silent after g and q	u	quero	KEH-rooh

Diphthongs

ai	Like ai in *thai*	ai	pai	pal
am	Like oa in *moan*	oan	falam	FAH-loan
ão	Like oa in *moan*	oan	coração	koo-rah-SOAN
au	Like ow in *owl*	ow	pausa	POW-zah
ei	Like ay in *bay*	ay	peixe	PAY-sh
em	Like aing in *saying*	ain	sabem	SAH-bain
eu	Like u in *university*	ew	euro	EW-roh
õe	Like oin in *loin*	oin	prisões	pri-ZOIN-sh
ói	Like oy in *toy*	oy	dói	doy
ou	Like au in *aubergine*	au	outro	AU-trooh
ua	Like whi in *while*	whi	quase	KWHI-z
ue	Like we in *wet*	we	frequente	freh-KWEN-t
ui	Like ui in *suite*	ooy	gratuito	gra-TOOY-too
uo	Like woa in *woah*	woa	aquoso	a-KWOAH-zoo

GENERAL VOCABULARY

first name
nome *m*
NOH-m

date of birth
data de nascimento
DAH-teh d na-she-MEN-tooh

place of birth
local de nascimento
loo-KALH d na-she-MEN-tooh

email address
endereço de e-mail
en-d-REH-sooh d i-MEHIL

phone number
número de telefone
NOO-meh-rooh d teh-leh-foh-n

last name
apelido
ah-p-LEE-dooh

age
idade
e-DAH-d

address	**morada**	moo-RAH-dah
marital status	**estado civil**	sh-TAH-dooh see-VEEL
children	**filhos**	FEE-lloos
home country	**país de origem**	pa-ISH d oh-REE-jem
place of residence	**local de residência**	loo-KAHL d rreh-zee-DEN-seeah
single	**solteiro** *m* / **solteira** *f*	sol-TAY-rooh / sol-TAY-rah
in a relationship	**numa relação**	NOO-mah rreh-lah-SOAN
divorced	**divorciado** *m* / **divorciada** *f*	dee-voor-see-AH-dooh / dee-voor-see-AH-dah
married	**casado** *m* / **casada** *f*	kah-ZAH-dooh / kah-ZAH-dah
widowed	**viúvo** *m* / **viúva** *f*	vee-OO-vooh / vee-OO-vah
What's your name?	**Como se chama?**	KOH-mooh s SHAH-mah?
Where are you from?	**De onde é?**	D ON-dh eh?
Where were you born?	**Onde nasceu?**	ON-dh nash-EW?
When were you born?	**Quando nasceu?**	kWAN-dooh nash-EW?
What is your address?	**Qual é a sua morada?**	kwahl eh ah suah mooh-RAH-dah?
What's your phone number?	**Qual é o seu número de telefone?**	kwahl eh ooh sew NOO-meh-rooh d teh-leh-FOH-n?
Are you married?	**É casado** *m* / **casada** *f*?	eh kah-ZAH-dooh / kah-ZAH-dah?
Do you have children?	**Tem filhos?**	tain FEE-lloosh?

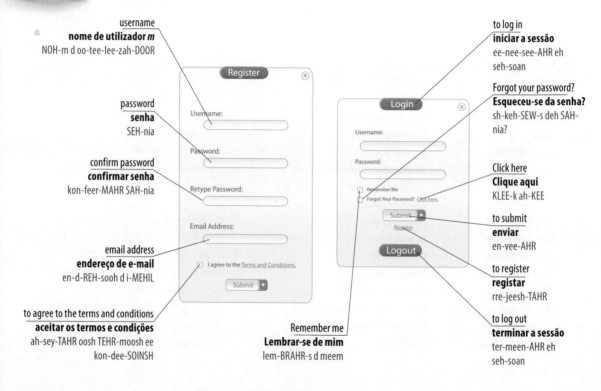

username
nome de utilizador _m_
NOH-m d oo-tee-lee-zah-DOOR

password
senha
SEH-nia

confirm password
confirmar senha
kon-feer-MAHR SAH-nia

email address
endereço de e-mail
en-d-REH-sooh d i-MEHL

to agree to the terms and conditions
aceitar os termos e condições
ah-sey-TAHR oosh TEHR-moosh ee
kon-dee-SOINSH

to log in
iniciar a sessão
ee-nee-see-AHR eh
seh-soan

Forgot your password?
Esqueceu-se da senha?
sh-keh-SEW-s deh SAH-nia?

Click here
Clique aqui
KLEE-k ah-KEE

to submit
enviar
en-vee-AHR

to register
registar
rre-jeesh-TAHR

to log out
terminar a sessão
ter-meen-AHR eh
seh-soan

Remember me
Lembrar-se de mim
lem-BRAHR-s d meem

1234567890

0	zero	**zero**	ZEH-rooh
1	one	**um**	oom
2	two	**dois**	doysh
3	three	**três**	trehsh
4	four	**quatro**	KWA-trooh
5	five	**cinco**	SEEN-kooh
6	six	**seis**	saysh
7	seven	**sete**	seht
8	eight	**oito**	oyt
9	nine	**nove**	NOH-v
10	ten	**dez**	dehsh
11	eleven	**onze**	onz
12	twelve	**doze**	DOH-z
13	thirteen	**treze**	TREH-z
14	fourteen	**catorze**	kah-TOHRZ
15	fifteen	**quinze**	KEEN-z
16	sixteen	**dezasseis**	deh-zah-SAYSH

17	seventeen	**dezassete**	deh-zah-SEHT
18	eighteen	**dezoito**	deh-ZOY-tooh
19	nineteen	**dezanove**	deh-zah-NOH-v
20	twenty	**vinte**	veent
21	twenty-one	**vinte e um**	veent ee oohm
30	thirty	**trinta**	TREEN-teh
40	forty	**quarenta**	kwa-REHN-tah
50	fifty	**cinquenta**	seen-KWEHN-tah
60	sixty	**sessenta**	ses-EHN-tah
70	seventy	**setenta**	seh-TEHN-tah
80	eighty	**oitenta**	oy-TEHN-tah
90	ninety	**noventa**	noh-VEHN-tah
100	one hundred	**cem**	sain
101	one hundred and one	**cento e um**	sentooh ee oohm?
1000	one thousand	**mil**	meel
1 000 000	one million	**um milhão**	oohm mee-LLOAN

1st (first)
primeiro
pree-MAY-rooh

2nd (second)
segundo
seh-GOOHN-dooh

3rd (third)
terceiro
ter-SAY-rooh

4th	fourth	**quarto**	KWAHR-tooh
5th	fifth	**quinto**	KEEN-tooh
6th	sixth	**sexto**	SAY-shtooh
7th	seventh	**sétimo**	SEH-teeh-mooh
8th	eighth	**oitavo**	oy-TAH-vooh
9th	ninth	**nono**	NOH-nooh
10th	tenth	**décimo**	DEH-see-mooh
11th	eleventh	**décimo primeiro**	DEH-see-mooh pree-MAY-rooh

12th	twelfth	**décimo segundo**	DEH-see-mooh seh-GOOHN-dooh
13th	thirteenth	**décimo terceiro**	DEH-see-mooh ter-SAY-rooh
14th	fourteenth	**décimo quarto**	DEH-see-mooh KWAHR-tooh
15th	fifteenth	**décimo quinto**	DEH-see-mooh KEEN-tooh
16th	sixteenth	**décimo sexto**	DEH-see-mooh SAY-shtooh
17th	seventeenth	**décimo sétimo**	DEH-see-mooh SEH-teeh-mooh
18th	eighteenth	**décimo oitavo**	DEH-see-mooh oy-TAH-vooh
19th	nineteenth	**décimo nono**	DEH-see-mooh NOH-nooh
20th	twentieth	**vigésimo**	veeh-JEH-zee-mooh
21st	twenty-first	**vigésimo primeiro**	vee-JEH-zee-mooh pree-MAY-rooh
22nd	twenty-second	**vigésimo segundo**	vee-JEH-zee-mooh seh-GOOHN-dooh
23rd	twenty-third	**vigésimo terceiro**	vee-JEH-zee-mooh ter-SAY-rooh
24th	twenty-fourth	**vigésimo quarto**	vee-JEH-zee-mooh KWAHR-tooh
25th	twenty-fifth	**vigésimo quinto**	vee-JEH-zee-mooh KEEN-tooh
26th	twenty-sixth	**vigésimo sexto**	vee-JEH-zee-mooh SAY-shtooh
27th	twenty-seventh	**vigésimo sétimo**	vee-JEH-zee-mooh SEH-teeh-mooh
28th	twenty-eighth	**vigésimo oitavo**	vee-JEH-zee-mooh oy-TAH-vooh
29th	twenty-ninth	**vigésimo nono**	vee-JEH-zeeh-mooh NOH-nooh
30th	thirtieth	**trigésimo**	tree-JEH-zeeh-mooh
40th	fortieth	**quadrigésimo**	kwah-dree-JEH-zeeh-mooh
50th	fiftieth	**quinquagésimo**	keen-kwah-JEH-zeeh-mooh
60th	sixtieth	**sexagésimo**	sex-ah-JEH-zeeh-mooh
70th	seventieth	**septuagésimo**	sep-tooh-ah-JEH-zeeh-mooh
80th	eightieth	**octogésimo**	oh-ktoh-JEH-zeeh-mooh
90th	ninetieth	**nonagésimo**	noh-nah-JEH-zeeh-mooh
100th	hundredth	**centésimo**	sen-TEH-zee-mooh

| noon | **meio-dia** | mayoo-deeah |
| midnight | **meia-noite** | mayah-NOY-t |

| one am | **uma da manhã** | oohmah dah mah-NIANI |
| one pm | **uma da tarde** | oomah dah TAHR-d |

| two am | **duas da manhã** | DOO-ahsh dah mah-NIAN |
| two pm | **duas da tarde** | DOO-ahsh dah TAHR-d |

| three am | **três da manhã** | trehsh dah mah-NIAN |
| three pm | **três da tarde** | trehsh dah TAHR-d |

| four am | **quatro da manhã** | KWA-trooh dah mah-NIAN |
| four pm | **quatro da tarde** | KWA-trooh dah TAHR-d |

| five am | **cinco da manhã** | SEEN-kooh dah mah-NIAN |
| five pm | **cinco da tarde** | SEEN-kooh dah TAHR-d |

| six am | **seis da manhã** | SAY-sh dah mah-NIAN |
| six pm | **seis da tarde** | SAY-sh dah TAHR-d |

| seven am | **sete da manhã** | seht dah mah-NIAN |
| seven pm | **sete da tarde** | seht dah TAHR-d |

| eight am | **oito da manhã** | oyt dah mah-NIAN |
| eight pm | **oito da noite** | oyt dah NOY-t |

| nine am | **nove da manhã** | NOH-v dah mah-NIAN |
| nine pm | **nove da noite** | NOH-v dah NOY-t |

| ten am | **dez da manhã** | dehsh dah mah-NIAN |
| ten pm | **dez da noite** | dehsh dah NOY-t |

| eleven am | **onze da manhã** | onz dah mah-NIAN |
| eleven pm | **onze da noite** | onz dah NOY-t |

quarter to
um quarto para as
oom KWAHR-too PAH-rah ahsh

ten to
dez para as
dehsh PAH-rah

five to
cinco para as
SEEN-kooh PAH-rah ahsh

. . . o'clock
hora
OH-rah

five past
e cinco
ee SEEN-kooh

ten past
e dez
ee dehsh

quarter past
e um quarto
ee oom KWAR-tooh

half past
e meia
ee MAY-ah

What time is it?	**Que horas são?**	keh OH-rash soan?
It's nine thirty.	**São nove e meia.**	soan NOH-v ee MAY-ah
Excuse me, could you tell me the time please?	**Desculpe, pode dizer-me que horas são?**	dsh-KOOL-p POH-d dee-ZEHR-m keh OH-rash soan?
It's about half past nine.	**São cerca de nove e meia.**	soan SEHR-KEH d NOH-v ee MAY-ah

Monday
Segunda-feira
seh-GOOHN-dah FAY-rah

Tuesday
Terça-feira
TEHR-sah FAY-rah

Wednesday
Quarta-feira
KWAR-tah FAY-rah

Thursday
Quinta-feira
KEEN-tah FAY-rah

Friday
Sexta-feira
SAYSH-tah FAY-rah

Saturday
Sábado
SAH-bah-dooh

Sunday
Domingo
dooh-MEEN-gooh

on Monday	**na segunda**	nah seh-GOOHN-dah
from Tuesday	**de terça**	deh TEHR-sah
until Wednesday	**a quarta**	ah KWAR-tah

JANUARY

January
janeiro
jah-NAY-rooh

FEBRUARY

February
fevereiro
f-v-RAY-rooh

MARCH

March
março
MAHR-sooh

APRIL

April
abril
ah-BREEL

MAY

May
maio
mahiooh

JUNE

June
junho
JOOH-niooh

JULY

July
julho
jooh-llooh

AUGUST

August
agosto
ah-GAUSH-tooh

SEPTEMBER

September
setembro
s-TEHM-brooh

OCTOBER

October
outubro
ow-TOOH-brooh

NOVEMBER

November
novembro
nooh-VEM-brooh

DECEMBER

December
dezembro
d-ZEM-brooh

in July	**em julho**	ain JOO-llooh
since September	**desde setembro**	DEHSH-d s-TEM-brooh
until October	**até outubro**	ah-TEH oh-TOOh-brooh
for two months	**durante dois meses**	dooh-RAN-t doysh MEH-zsh

morning	late morning	noon	afternoon	evening	night
manhã	**fim da manhã**	**meio-dia**	**tarde**	**noite**	**madrugada**
mah-NIAN	feem dah mah-NIAN	mayoo-deeah	TAHR-d	NOY-t	mah-drooh-GAH-dah

in the morning	**de manhã**	d mah-NIAN
in the evening	**à noite**	ah NOY-t
in the night	**de madrugada**	d mah-drooh-GAH-dah

ATM / cashpoint
caixa multibanco
KAY-shah mool-tee-BAN-kooh

cash
dinheiro
dee-NIAY-rooh

bank statement
extrato bancário
esh-TRAH-tooh bahn-KAH-ree-ooh

cheque
cheque
shek

account	**conta**	KON-tah
bank	**banco**	BAN-kooh
bank charges	**comissões bancárias** *f*	kooh-mee-SOINSH ban-KAH-ree-ash
debit card	**cartão de débito**	kar-TOAN d DEB-ee-tooh
debt	**dívida**	DEE-vee-dah
current account	**conta corrente**	KON-teh kooh-RREN-t
loan	**empréstimo**	em-PRESH-tee-mooh
mortgage	**hipoteca**	ee-pooh-TEH-kah
savings account	**conta poupança**	KON-tah poh-PAN-sah
standing order	**ordem permanente**	OHR-daym per-mah-NEN-t
to borrow money	**pedir um empréstimo**	p-deer oom em-PRESH-tee-mooh
to invest	**investir**	een-vehsh-TEER
to lend money	**emprestar dinheiro**	em-presh-TAHR dee-NIAY-rooh
to pay	**pagar**	pah-GAHR
to take out a loan	**pedir um empréstimo**	p-DEER oom em-PRESH-tee-mooh
to withdraw from the account	**levantar da conta**	I-vahn-TAHR dah KON-tah
to take out a mortgage	**pedir uma hipoteca**	p-DEER oomah ee-pooh-TEH-kah
to withdraw	**levantar**	I-vahn-TAHR

credit card
cartão de crédito
kahr-TOAN d KREH-dee-tooh

to save
poupar
pau-PAHR

Pound Sterling
Libra Esterlina
LEE-brah esh-tehr-LEE-nah

Euro
Euro
EW-roh

Dollar
Dólar
DOH-lahr

Franc
Franco
FRAN-kooh

Yen
Iene *m*
IEH-n

Won
Won
wohn

Yuan
Yuan
Ioo-AHN

Indian Rupee
Rupia Indiana
RrOOH-pee-ah een-dee-AH-nah

Zloty
Zloti
ZLOH-tee

Ruble
Rublo
Rroo-bloh

Leu
Leu
leooh

Forint
Forint
FOH-reent

Krone	**Coroa**	Koo-ROH-ah	exchange rate	**taxa de câmbio**	TAH-shah d KAM-bee-ooh
Peso	**Peso**	PEH-zooh	exchange rate for US Dollars to Japanese Yen	**taxa de câmbio de dólares americanos para ienes japoneses**	TAH-shah d KAM-bee-ooh d DOH-lah-rsh ah-meh-ree-KA-noosh PAH-rah YE-nsh jah-pooh-NEH-zsh
Pound	**Libra**	LEE-brah			
Dinar	**Dinar**	Dee-NAHR	foreign exchange	**câmbio internacional**	KAM-bee-ooh een-tehr-nah-see-ooh-NAHL
Shilling	**Xelim**	Sh-LEEM			
Dirham	**Dirham**	Deer-AHM	foreign exchange rate	**taxa de câmbio internacional**	TAH-shah d KAM-bee-ooh een-tehr-nah-see-ooh-NAHL
Rial	**Rial**	Rree-AHL			
Dong	**Dong**	dong			

 PEOPLE

a middle-aged man
um homem de meia idade
oom OH-main d MAY-ah ee-DAH-d

an old man
um idoso
oom ee-DOH-zooh

a young man
um jovem
oom JOH-vain

a young woman
uma mulher jovem
ooma moo-LLER JOH-vain

baby
bebé
beh-BEH

a teenage boy
um adolescente
oom ah-dooh-lesh-SEN-t

a young boy
um rapazinho
oom rrah-pah-ZEE-niooh

a teenage girl
uma adolescente
ooma ah-dooh-lesh-SEN-t

teenager	**adolescente**	ah-dooh-lesh-SEN-t
a young girl	**uma rapariga nova**	ooma rrah-pah-REE-gah NOH-vah
a seven-year-old girl	**uma menina de sete anos**	ooma meh-NEE-nah d set AH-noosh
young	**novo**	NOH-voh
middle-aged	**meia idade**	MAY-ah ee-DAH-d
old	**velho**	VEH-llooh
adult	**adulto**	ah-DOOL-too
She is forty years old.	**Ela tem quarenta anos.**	EH-lah tain kwa-REN-tah A-noosh
She is in her thirties.	**Ela está na casa dos trinta.**	EH-lah sh-TAH nah KAH-zah
She is about twenty.	**Ela tem uns vinte anos.**	EH-lah tain oonsh VEEN-t A-noosh
child	**uma criança**	ooma kree-AN-sah
a little boy	**um menino**	oom meh-NEE-nooh
a little girl	**uma menina**	ooma meh-NEE-nah
He is six years old.	**Ele tem seis anos.**	EH-l tain SAY-sh A-noosh

a beautiful girl
uma rapariga linda
ooma rrah-pah-REE-gah
LEEN-dah

a pretty woman
uma mulher bonita
ooma moo-LLER booh-NEE-tah

a handsome man
um homem bonito
oom OH-main booh-NEE-tooh

attractive	atrativo	ah-trah-TEE-vooh
beautiful	lindo	LEEN-dooh
cute	engraçado	en-grah-SAH-dooh
handsome	bonito	booh-NEE-tooh
ugly	feio	FAY-ooh
unattractive	pouco atrativo	POH-kooh ah-trah-TEE-vooh
casually dressed	vestido casualmente	v-sh-TEE-dooh kah-zooh-ahl-MEN-t

dirty	sujo	SOOH-jooh
elegant	elegante	ee-I-GAN-t
pretty	bonito	booh-NEE-tooh
fashionable	moderno	mooh-DEHR-nooh
neat	limpo	LEEM-pooh
poorly dressed	mal vestido	mahl v-sh-TEE-dooh
untidy	desleixado	dsh-lay-SHAH-dooh
well-dressed	bem vestido	bain v-sh-TEE-dooh

She is taller than him.	**Ela é mais alta do que ele.**	eh-lah eh maish AHL-tah dooh q EH-l
He isn't as tall as her.	**Ele não é tão alto como ela.**	eh-l noan eh toan AHL-rooh KOH-mooh EH-lah
She is of average height.	**Ela é de estatura média.**	eh-lah eh d sh-tah-TOOH-rah MEH-dee-ah

very tall
muito alto
MOOIN-tooh AHL-tooh

tall
alto
AHL-tooh

quite tall
bastante alto
bash-TAN-t AHL-tooh

not very tall
não muito alto
noan MOOIN-tooh AHL-tooh

short
baixo
BAI-shoo

thin	slim	plump	fat
magro	**magro**	**roliço**	**gordo**
MAH-grooh	MAH-grooh	rooh-LEE-sooh	GOHR-dooh

slender	**esbelto**	j-BEL-tooh
skinny	**magricela**	mah-gree-SEH-lah
obese	**obeso**	oh-BEH-zooh
underweight	**peso a menos**	PEH-zooh ah MEH-noosh
overweight	**excesso de peso**	esh-SEH-zooh d PEH-zooh
She is overweight / underweight.	**Ela tem excesso de peso / peso a menos.**	EH-lah tain esh-SEH-zooh d PEH-zooh / PEH-zooh ah MEH-noosh
to lose weight	**perder peso**	per-DEHR PEH-zooh

grey
grisalho
gree-ZAH-llooh

red
ruivo
ROOI-vooh

dark
escuro
esh-KOO-rooh

black
preto
PREH-tooh

blond
loiro
LOI-rooh

light
claro
CLAH-rooh

chestnut
castanho-claro
cash-TA-nio CLAH-rooh

brown
castanho
cash-TA-nio

straight
liso
LEE-zooh

curly
caracóis
kah-rah-KOHISH

wavy
ondulado
on-dooh-LAH-dooh

thick
espesso
sh-PEH-sooh

bald
careca
kah-REH-kah

long
comprido
kom-PREE-dooh

short
curto
KOOHR-tooh

shoulder-length
pelo ombro
PEH-looh OMH-brooh

medium-length
comprimento médio
kom-pree-MEN-tooh MEH-dee-ooh

a brunette	**uma morena**	OOH-mah moh-REH-nah
a redhead	**uma ruiva**	OOH-mah ROOI-vah
a blonde	**uma loira**	OOH-mah LOI-rah
a dark-haired woman	**uma mulher com cabelo escuro**	OOH-mah moo-llehr kom kah-BEH-looh sh-KOOH-rooh
He has long dark hair.	**Ele tem cabelo escuro comprido.**	EH-I tain kah-BEH-looh sh-KOOH-rooh kom-PREE-dooh
He has curly hair.	**Ele tem caracóis.**	EH-I tain kah-rah-KOHISH
He is bald.	**Ele é careca.**	EH-I eh kah-REH-kah

eyebrows	eyelashes
sobrancelhas	**pestanas**
soo-bran-SEH-llash	psh-TAH-nahsh

glasses
óculos
OH-kooh-loosh

sunglasses
óculos escuros
OH-kooh-loosh sh-KOOH-roosh

blue	**azuis**	ah-ZOOISH
grey	**cinzentos**	seen-ZEN-toosh
green	**verdes**	VEHR-dsh
brown	**castanhos**	kahsh-TAH-nioosh
dark	**escuros**	sh-KOOH-roosh
light	**claros**	KLAH-roosh

short sighted	**míope**	MEE-oohp
blind	**cego**	SEH-gooh
She wears glasses.	**Ela usa óculos.**	EH-lah OOH-zah OH-kooh-loosh
She has blue eyes.	**Ela tem olhos azuis.**	EH-lah tain OH-lloosh ah-ZOOISH
His eyes are dark brown.	**Os olhos dele são castanho-escuros.**	oosh OH-lloosh DEH-I soan kahsh-TAH-niooh sh-KOOH-roosh

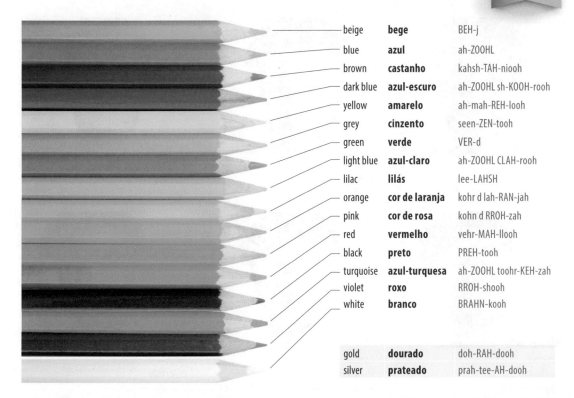

beige	**bege**	BEH-j
blue	**azul**	ah-ZOOHL
brown	**castanho**	kahsh-TAH-niooh
dark blue	**azul-escuro**	ah-ZOOHL sh-KOOH-rooh
yellow	**amarelo**	ah-mah-REH-looh
grey	**cinzento**	seen-ZEN-tooh
green	**verde**	VER-d
light blue	**azul-claro**	ah-ZOOHL CLAH-rooh
lilac	**lilás**	lee-LAHSH
orange	**cor de laranja**	kohr d lah-RAN-jah
pink	**cor de rosa**	kohn d RROH-zah
red	**vermelho**	vehr-MAH-llooh
black	**preto**	PREH-tooh
turquoise	**azul-turquesa**	ah-ZOOHL toohr-KEH-zah
violet	**roxo**	RROH-shooh
white	**branco**	BRAHN-kooh

gold	**dourado**	doh-RAH-dooh
silver	**prateado**	prah-tee-AH-dooh

33

positive
otimista
oh-tee-MEESH-tah

stubborn
teimoso
tay-MOH-zooh

lucky
sortudo
soor-TOOH-dooh

dreamer
sonhador
sooh-NIAH-door

visionary
visionário
vee-zee-ooh-NAH-ree-ooh

funny
divertido
dee-vehr-TEE-dooh

talkative
falador
fah-lah-DOHR

energetic
energético
ee-ner-JEH-tee-kooh

negative
pessimista
peh-see-MEESH-tah

creative	**criativo**	kree-ah-TEE-vooh
adventurous	**aventureiro**	ah-ven-tooh-RAY-rooh
kind	**bondoso**	bon-DOH-zooh
calm	**calmo**	KAHL-mooh
caring	**atencioso**	ah-ten-see-OH-zooh
punctual	**pontual**	POHN-tooh-ahl
crazy	**maluco**	mah-LOOH-kooh
liar	**mentiroso**	mehn-tee-ROH-zooh
frank	**sincero**	seen-SEH-rooh
strong	**forte**	FOHR-t

grandparents
avós
ah-VOHSH

aunt
tia
teeah

uncle
tio
teeooh

parents
pais
pahish

sister-in-law
cunhada
kooh-NIAH-dah

family
família
fah-MEE-lee-ah

sister
irmã
eer-MAN

brother
irmão
eer-MOAN

cousin
primo
PREE-mooh

nephew
sobrinho
sooh-bree-niooh

niece
sobrinha
sooh-bree-niah

myself
eu próprio
ew PROH-pree-ooh

wife
mulher
moo-LLEHR

grandchildren	**netos**	NEH-toosh
daughter	**filha**	FEE-llah
father	**pai**	pahi
father-in-law	**sogro**	SOH-grooh
grandchild	**neto**	NEH-tooh
granddaughter	**neta**	NEH-tah
grandfather	**avô**	ah-VAUH
grandmother	**avó**	ah-VOH
grandson	**neto**	NEH-toosh
great-grandparents	**bisavós**	bee-zah-VOHSH
husband	**marido**	mah-REE-dooh
mother	**mãe**	main
mother-in-law	**sogra**	SOH-grah
son	**filho**	FEE-llooh
twin brother	**irmão gémeo**	eer-MOAN JEH-mee-ooh
brother-in-law	**cunhado**	koo-NIAH-dooh

single child
filho único
FEE-llooh OOH-nee-kooh

family with two children
família com dois filhos
fah-MEE-lee-ah kom doish FEE-lloosh

big family
família numerosa
fah-MEE-lee-ah nooh-meh-ROH-zah

childless
sem filhos
sain FEE-lloosh

single father
pai solteiro
pahi sol-TAY-rooh

single mother
mãe solteira
main sol-TAY-rah

adoption
adoção
ah-doh-SOAN

orphan
órfão *m* / **órfã** *f*
OHR-foan / OHR-fan

widow
viúva
vee-OOH-vah

stepfather	**padrasto**	pah-DRASH-tooh
stepmother	**madrasta**	mah-DRASH-tah
to be pregnant	**estar grávida**	sh-TAHR GRAH-vee-dah
to expect a baby	**estar à espera de bebé**	sh-TAHR ah sh-PEH-rah d beh-BEH
to give birth to	**dar à luz**	dahr ah loosh
born	**nascido** *m* / **nascida** *f*	nash-SEE-dooh / nash-SEE-dah
to baptise	**batizar**	bah-tee-ZAHR
to raise	**criar**	kree-AHR

to be engaged	**estar noivo**	sh-TAHR NOI-vooh
to marry	**casar-se**	kah-ZAHR-s
to be married to	**estar casado** *m* / **casada** *f*	sh-TAHR kah-ZAH-dooh / kah-ZAH-dah
divorced	**divorciado** *m* / **divorciada** *f*	dee-voohr-see-AH-dooh / dee-voohr-see-AH-dah
widowed	**viúvo** *m* / **viúva** *f*	vee-OOH-vooh / vee-OOH-vah
widower	**viúvo**	vee-OOH-vooh
to die	**morrer**	moo-RREHR

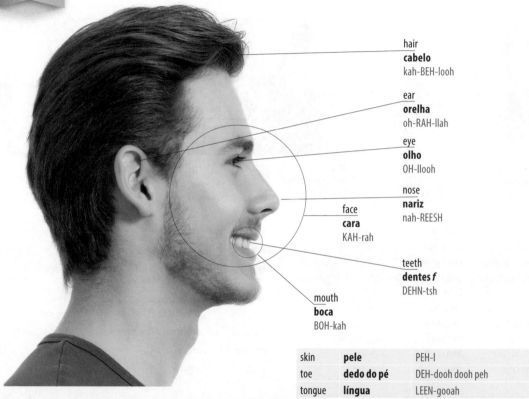

hair
cabelo
kah-BEH-looh

ear
orelha
oh-RAH-llah

eye
olho
OH-llooh

nose
nariz
nah-REESH

face
cara
KAH-rah

teeth
dentes *f*
DEHN-tsh

mouth
boca
BOH-kah

skin	**pele**	PEH-I
toe	**dedo do pé**	DEH-dooh dooh peh
tongue	**língua**	LEEN-gooah

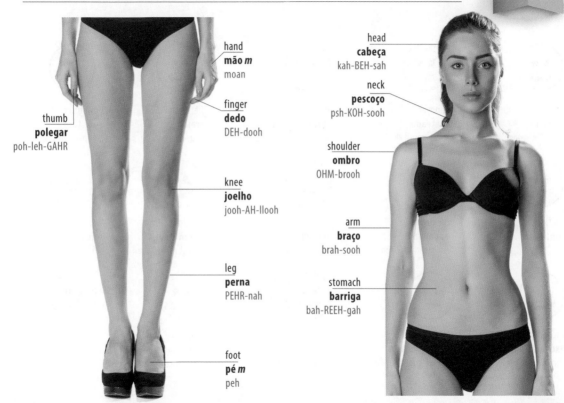

hand
mão *m*
moan

finger
dedo
DEH-dooh

thumb
polegar
poh-leh-GAHR

knee
joelho
jooh-AH-llooh

leg
perna
PEHR-nah

foot
pé *m*
peh

head
cabeça
kah-BEH-sah

neck
pescoço
psh-KOH-sooh

shoulder
ombro
OHM-brooh

arm
braço
brah-sooh

stomach
barriga
bah-REEH-gah

angry
zangado
zahn-GAH-dooh

annoyed
chateado
shah-tee-AH-dooh

ashamed
envergonhado
en-ver-goo-NIAH-dooh

betrayed
traído
trah-EE-dooh

confused
confuso
kon-FOOH-zooh

confident
confiante
kon-fee-AHN-t

cheated
enganado
en-gah-NAH-dooh

depressed
deprimido
deh-pree-MEE-dooh

delighted
encantado
en-kahn-TAH-dooh

disappointed
desiludido
deh-zee-looh-DEE-dooh

excited
excitado
shee-TAH-dooh

embarrassed
envergonhado
en-ver-goo-NIAH-dooh

furious
furioso
foo-ree-OH-soh

frightened
assustado
ah-soosh-TAH-dooh

happy
feliz
f-LEESH

horrified
horrorizado
oh-rroh-ree-ZAH-dooh

irritated
irritado
ee-rree-TAH-dooh

intrigued
intrigado
een-tree-GAH-dooh

jealous
com ciúmes
kom see-OOH-msh

lazy
preguiçoso
pre-ghee-SOH-zooh

lucky
sortudo
sor-TOOH-dooh

relaxed
relaxado
reh-lah-SHAH-dooh

sad
triste
TREE-sht

stressed
preocupado
pree-oh-koo-PAH-dooh

terrified
assustado
ah-soosh-TAH-dooh

upset
chateado
shah-teh-AH-dooh

unhappy
infeliz
een-f-LEESH

43

hobby	My hobby is ...	**O meu hobby é ...**	ooh mehu hobby eh
hobby	Are you interested in ...?	**Interessas-te por...?**	een-t-REH-sash-t poohr
obi			

baking
fazer bolos
fah-ZEHR BOH-loosh

coin collecting
colecionar moedas
ko-leh-see-ooh-NAHR mooh-eh-dash

woodworking
carpintaria
kahr-peen-tah-REE-ah

stamp collecting
filatelia
fee-lah-t-LEE-ah

cooking
cozinhar
koo-zee-NIAHR

dance
dançar
dan-SAHR

drawing
desenhar
d-z-NIAHR

reading
ler
lehr

jewellery making
joalharia
jooh-ah-llah-REE-ah

knitting
tricot
tree-KOH

painting
pintar
peen-TAHR

sewing
costura
kosh-TOOH-rah

45

badminton
badmington
bahd-MEEN-tohn

bowling
bowling
BOHW-leeng

boxing
boxe
box

chess
xadrez
shah-DRESH

cycling
ciclismo
see-KLEESH-mooh

darts
dardos
dahr-doosh

diving
mergulho
mehr-GOOH-llooh

fishing
pesca
PESH-kah

football
futebol
foot-BALL

orienteering
orientação *f*
oh-ree-en-tah-SOAN

gymnastics
ginástica
gee-NAHSH-tee-kah

handball
andebol
ande-BALL

jogging
jogging
jog-EENG

kayaking
canoagem *f*
kah-nooh-AH-jain

martial arts
artes marciais
AHR-tsh mar-see-AISH

mountain biking
ciclismo de montanha
see-KLEESH-mooh d mohn-
TAH-niah

paintball
paintball
paint-BALL

photography
fotografia
fooh-tooh-grah-FEE-ah

47

rock climbing
escalada
sh-kah-LAH-dah

running
correr
kooh-rrehr

sailing
vela
VEH-lah

surfing
surf
surf

swimming
natação *f*
nah-tah-SOAN

table tennis
ténis de mesa
TEH-neesh d MEH-zah

travel
viajar
vee-ah-JAHR

tennis
ténis
TEH-neesh

yoga
ioga *m*
ee-OH-gah

I like to swim.	**Gosto de nadar.**	GOH-shtooh d nah-DAHR.
What activities do you like to do?	**O que gostas de praticar?**	ooh k GOH-shtash d prah-tee-KAHR

to get up
acordar
ah-koor-DAHR

to take a shower
tomar um duche
tooh-MAHR oohm DOOH-sh

to brush your teeth
lavar os dentes
lah-VAHR oosh DEN-tsh

to floss your teeth
usar fio dentário
ooh-ZAHR feehoo dehn-TAH-ree-ooh

to shave
fazer a barba
fah-ZEHR ah BAHR-bah

to brush your hair
pentear-se
pen-tee-AHR-s

to put on makeup
maquilhar-se
mah-kee-LLAHR-s

to get dressed
vestir-se
vsh-TEER-s

to get undressed
despir-se
dsh-PEER-s

to take a bath
tomar banho
tooh-MAHR bah-niooh

to go to bed
ir para a cama
eer PAH-rah ah KAH-mah

to sleep
dormir
doohr-MEER

Valentine's Day
Dia dos Namorados *m*
deeah doosh nah-mooh-
RAH-doosh

graduation
formatura
fohr-mah-TOOH-rah

Easter
Páscoa
PAHSH-kooh-ah

engagement
noivado
noy-VAH-dooh

marriage
casamento
kah-zah-MEHN-tooh

bride
noiva
NOY-vah

Christmas
Natal
nah-TAHL

Santa Claus / Father Christmas
Pai Natal
pahee nah-TAHL

candle
vela
VEH-lah

decoration
decoração f
deh-kooh-rah-SOAN

mistletoe
visco
VEESH-kooh

present / gift
presente m
preh-ZEHN-t

champagne
champanhe m
sham-PAHN-nieh

fireworks
fogo-de-artifício
FOH-gooh d ahr-tee-FEE-see-ooh

Advent calendar
Calendário de Advento
kah-len-DAH-ree-ooh d ad-VEHN-tooh

party
festa
FEH-shtah

birthday
aniversário
ah-nee-ver-SAH-ree-ooh

ceremony
cerimónia
seh-ree-MOH-nee-ah

wedding ring
aliança
ah-lee-AN-sah

decorated eggs
ovos decorados
OH-voosh deh-kooh-RAH-doosh

Easter Bunny
Coelhinho da Páscoa
kooh-eh-LLEE-nio dah PAHSH-kooh-ah

New Year	**Ano Novo**	AH-noo NOH-vooh
Happy New Year!	**Feliz Ano Novo!**	f-LEESH AH-noo NOH-vooh
Happy Birthday!	**Parabéns!**	pah-rab-BAYNSH
All the best!	**Tudo de bom!**	TOO-dooh d boan

Congratulations!	**Parabéns!**	pah-rab-BAYNSH
Good luck!	**Boa sorte!**	boah SOH-rt
Merry Christmas!	**Feliz Natal!**	f-LEESH nah-TAHL
Happy Easter!	**Feliz Páscoa!**	f-LEESH PAHSH-kooh-ah

Christianity
Cristianismo
kreesh-tee-ah-NEESH-mooh

Confucianism
Confucionismo
kon-fooh-see-ooh-
NEESH-mooh

Jainism
Jainismo
jay-NEESH-mooh

Islam
Islão
eesh-LOAN

Buddhism
Budismo
booh-DEESH-mooh

Judaism
Judaísmo
jooh-dah-EESH-mooh

Hinduism
Hinduísmo
een-dooh-EESH-mooh

Taoism
Taoísmo
tah-ooh-EESH-mooh

Sikhism
Siquismo
see-KEESH-mooh

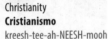

to confess	**professar**	prooh-f-SAHR
without religious confession	**sem confissão religiosa**	sain kon-fee-SOAN rrh-lee-jee-OH-zah
to believe in God	**acreditar em Deus**	ah-kr-deeh-TAHR ain DE-oosh
to have faith	**ter fé**	tehr feh
to pray	**rezar**	rrh-ZAHR

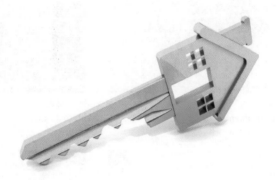

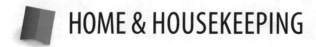

HOME & HOUSEKEEPING

house
casa
KAH-zah

flat
apartamento
ah-pahr-tah-MEN-tooh

block of flats
bloco de apartamentos
BLOH-kooh d ah-pahr-tah-MEN-toosh

duplex / two-storey house
duplex
dooh-PLEX

detached house
moradia
mooh-rah-DEE-ah

co-ownership
co-propriedade
koh-proh-pree-ah-DAH-d

houseboat
casa flutuante
KAH-zah flooh-tooh-AHN-t

caravan
caravana
kah-rah-VAH-nah

farm
quinta
KEEN-tah

flatshare
apartamento partilhado
ah-pahr-tah-MEN-tooh pahr-tee-LLAH-dooh

Where do you live?	**Onde moras?**	OH-nd MOH-rash?
I live in a flatshare.	**Moro num apartamento partilhado.**	MOH-rooh noohm ah-pahr-tah-MEHN-tooh pahr-tee-LLAH-dooh
I live with my parents.	**Vivo com os meus pais.**	VEE-vooh kom oosh meush pahish

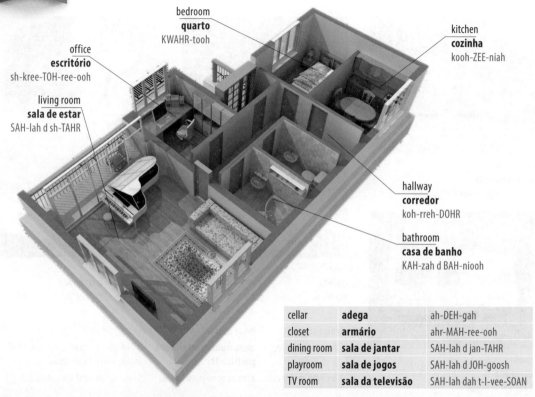

bedroom
quarto
KWAHR-tooh

kitchen
cozinha
kooh-ZEE-niah

office
escritório
sh-kree-TOH-ree-ooh

living room
sala de estar
SAH-lah d sh-TAHR

hallway
corredor
koh-rreh-DOHR

bathroom
casa de banho
KAH-zah d BAH-niooh

cellar	**adega**	ah-DEH-gah
closet	**armário**	ahr-MAH-ree-ooh
dining room	**sala de jantar**	SAH-lah d jan-TAHR
playroom	**sala de jogos**	SAH-lah d JOH-goosh
TV room	**sala da televisão**	SAH-lah dah t-I-vee-SOAN

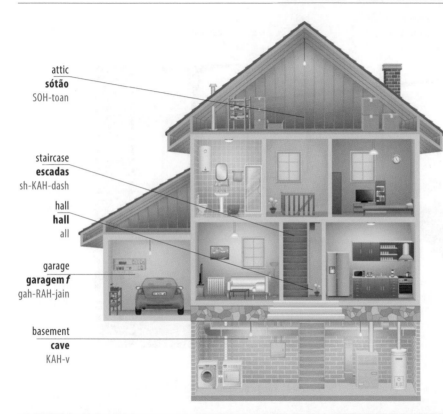

attic
sótão
SOH-toan

staircase
escadas
sh-KAH-dash

hall
hall
all

garage
garagem *f*
gah-RAH-jain

basement
cave
KAH-v

porch
alpendre *m*
ahl-PEHN-dr

patio
pátio
PAH-teeooh

workshop
oficina
oh-fee-SEE-nah

window
janela
jah-NEH-lah

bed
cama
KAH-mah

lamp
candeeiro
kan-dee-AY-rooh

pillow
almofada
al-mooh-FAH-dah

blanket
cobertor
kooh-br-TOHR

bedsheet
lençóis
len-SOHISH

chest of drawers
cómoda
KOH-mooh-dah

carpet
tapete *m*
tah-PEH-t

bedroom
quarto
KWARH-tooh

bed linen   **roupa de cama**   RROH-pah d KAH-mah

bathroom
casa de banho
KAH-zah d BAH-niooh

toilet
sanita
sah-NEE-tah

bidet
bidé *m*
bee-DEH

mirror
espelho
sh-PAY-llooh

shower
chuveiro
shooh-VAY-rooh

tap
torneira
toohr-NAY-rah

bath towel
toalha de banho
too-AH-llah d BAH-niooh

wash basin
lavatório
lah-vah-TOH-ree-ooh

bath
banho
BAH-niooh

flush
autoclismo
au-toh-see-KLEESH-mooh

comb
pente *m*
PEN-t

soap
sabonete *m*
sah-booh-NEH-t

dental floss
fio dentário
feeooh den-TAH-ree-ooh

sponge
esponja
sh-PON-jah

rubbish bin
caixote do lixo *m*
kai-SHOT dooh
LEE-shooh

face cloth
toalha de rosto
too-AH-llah d ROSH-tooh

bathrobe
robe *m*
ROH-b

hairbrush
escova de cabelo
sh-KOH-vah d ka-BEH-looh

hair dryer
secador
s-kah-DOHR

hand towel
toalha de mãos
too-AH-llah d moansh

towel
toalha
too-AH-llah

razor
lâmina de barbear
LAH-mee-nah d bahr-bee-AHR

shaving cream
espuma de barbear
sh-POOH-mah d bahr-hee-AHR

toothbrush
escova de dentes
sh-KOH-vah d DEN-tsh

shampoo
champô
sham-POH

conditioner
condicionador
kon-dee-see-ooh-nah-DOHR

toothpaste
pasta de dentes
PAH-shtah d DEN-tsh

nail clippers
corta-unhas *m*
KOHT-tah OOH-niash

paper towel
papel de mãos
pah-PEHL d moansh

toilet paper
papel higiénico
pah-PEL ee-jee-EH-nee-kooh

fridge
frigorífico
free-gooh-REE-fee-kooh

microwave
micro-ondas
MEE-kroh OHN-dash

stove
fogão
fooh-GOAN

coffee machine
máquina de café
MAH-kee-nah d ka-FEH

freezer
congelador
kon-jeh-LAH-dohr

dishwasher
**máquina de
lavar loiça**
MAH-kee-nah
d lah-VAHR
LOY-sah

washing machine
máquina de lavar roupa
MAH-kee-nah d lah-VAHR
RROH-pah

oven
forno
FOHR-nooh

kettle
chaleira
shah-LAY-rah

toaster
torradeira
too-rrah-DAY-rah

cookery book
livro de culinária
LEE-vrooh d kooh-lee-NAH-ree-ah

dishcloth
pano da loiça
PAH-noo dah LOY-sah

draining board
escorredor
sh-kooh-rrh-DOHR

kitchen roll
papel de cozinha
pah-PEHL d kooh-ZEE-niah

plug
tampão
tam-poan

tea towel
pano de cozinha
PAH-nooh d kooh-ZEE-niah

shelf
prateleira
prah-t-LAY-rah

sink
lava-loiças
LAH-vah LOY-sash

tablecloth
toalha de mesa
too-AH-llah d MEH-zah

bottle opener
abre-cápsulas *m*
AH-br KAH-psooh-lash

chopping board
tábua de cortar
TAH-booah d koohr-TAHR

colander
escorredor
sh-kooh-rrh-DOHR

frying pan
frigideira
free-gee-DAY-rah

grater
ralador
rrah-lah-DOHR

juicer
máquina de sumos
MAH-kee-nah d SOOH-moosh

corkscrew
saca-rolhas
SAH-kah RROH-llash

kitchen scales
balança de cozinha
bah-LAN-sah d koo-ZEE-niah

mixing bowl
tigela
tee-JEH-lah

sieve
coador
kooh-ah-DOHR

saucepan
panela
pah-NEH-lah

whisk
batedor
bah-t-DOHR

tin opener
abre-latas *m*
AH-br LAH-tash

washing-up liquid
detergente *m*
d-tehr-JEN-t

to do the dishes / to do the washing up	**lavar a loiça**	lah-VAHR ah LOY-sah
to do the washing	**lavar a loiça**	lah-VAHR ah LOY-sah
to clear the table	**levantar a mesa**	l-vahn-TAHR ah MEH-zah
to set the table	**pôr a mesa**	poor ah MEH-zah

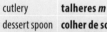

cutlery	**talheres** *m*	ta-LLEH-rsh
dessert spoon	**colher de sobremesa** *f*	koo-LLEHR d soo-breh-MEH-zah
soup spoon	**concha de sopa**	KON-shah d SOH-pah
spoon	**colher** *f*	koo-LLEHR

tablespoon
colher de sopa *f*
koo-LLEHR d SOH-pah

fork
garfo
GAHR-fooh

knife
faca
FAH-kah

teaspoon
colher de chá *f*
koo-LLEHR d shah

coffee spoon
colher de café *f*
koo-LLEHR d kah-FEH

plate
prato
PRAH-tooh

mug
caneca
kah-NEH-kah

sugar dispenser
açucareiro
ah-sooh-kah-RAY-rooh

jug
jarro
JAH-rrooh

saucer
pires *m*
PEE-rsh

cup
chávena
SHAH-v-nah

wine glass
copo de vinho
KOH-pooh d VEE-niooh

teapot
bule *m*
BOOH-l

bowl
tigela
tee-JEH-lah

jar
frasco
FRAH-shkooh

| crockery | **loiça** | LOY-sah |
| glass | **copo** | KOH-pooh |

armchair
cadeirão *m*
kah-day-ROAN

sofa
sofá *m*
sooh-FAH

lampshade
abajur
ah-bah-JOOHR

lamp
candeeiro
kan-dee-AY-rooh

vase
jarro
jah-rrooh

rug
tapete *m*
tah-PEH-t

bookcase
estante
sh-TAN-t

shelf
prateleira
prah-t-LAY-rah

plant
planta
PLAN-tah

picture
quadro
KWAH-drooh

table
mesa
MEH-zah

chair
cadeira
kah-DAY-rah

I can relax here.	**Aqui posso relaxar-me.**	ah-KEEH POH-sooh r-lah-SHAHR-m
Do you watch TV often?	**Vês muita televisão?**	vesh MOOY-tah t-l-vee-ZOAN
What is the size of the living room?	**Qual é o tamanho da sala de estar?**	kwal eh ooh tah-MAH-niooh dah SAH-lah d sh-TAHR?

hair dryer
secador
s-kah-DOHR

iron
ferro de engomar
FEH-rrooh d en-gooh-MAHR

radio
rádio
RAH-dee-ooh

washing machine
máquina de lavar roupa
MAH-kee-nah d lah-
VAHR RROH-pah

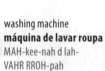

television
televisor
t-I-vee-ZOOHR

telephone
telefone *m*
t-I-FOH-n

cooker
fogão
fooh-GOAN

vacuum cleaner
aspirador
ash-pee-rah-
DOHR

mobile
telemóvel
teh-leh-MOH-
vehl

microwave
micro-ondas
MEE-kroh OHN-dash

kettle
chaleira
shah-LAY-rah

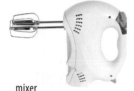

mixer
batedeira
bah-t-DAY-rah

refrigerator
frigorífico
free-gooh-REE-fee-kooh

gas oven
forno a gás
FOHR-nooh ah GASH

coffee grinder
moinho de café
mooh-EE-niooh d kah-FEH

juicer
máquina de sumos
MAH-kee-nah d SOO-moosh

sewing machine
máquina de costura
MAH-kee-nah d kosh-TOOH-rah

razor
máquina de barbear
MAH-kee-nah d bahr-bee-AHR

blender
varinha mágica
vah-REE-niah MAH-jee-kah

to clean up
limpar
leem-PAHR
74

to dust
limpar o pó
leem-PAHR ooh poh

to clean the floor
limpar o chão
leem-PAHR ooh shoan

to make the bed
fazer a cama
fah-ZEHR ah KAH-mah

to vacuum
aspirar
ash-pee-RAHR

to do the washing/laundry
lavar a roupa
lah-VAHR ah RROH-pah

to hang up the laundry
pendurar a roupa
pen-dooh-RAHR ah RROH-pah

to clean the windows
lavar as janelas
lah-VAHR ash jah-NEH-lash

to do the dishes
lavar a loiça
lah-VAHR ah LOY-sah

to iron
passar a ferro
pah-SAHR ah FEH-rroh

bucket
balde *m*
BAHL-d

dust cloth
pano do pó
PAH-nooh dooh poh

feather duster
espanador
sh-pahn-nah-DOHR

dustpan
pá
pah

mop
esfregona
sh-fr-GOH-nah

broom
vassoura
vah-SOH-rah

clothes line
estendal
sh-ten-DAHL

peg
mola da roupa
MOH-lah dah RROH-pah

paper towel
papel de cozinha
pah-PEHL d koo-ZEE-niah

laundry basket
cesto da roupa suja
SESH-tooh dah RROH-pah SOOH-jah

scrubbing brush
escova para a loiça
sh-KOH-vah PAH-rah ah LOY-sah

window cleaner
limpa-vidros
LEEM-pah VEE-droosh

sponge
esponja
sh-PON-jah

detergent
detergente *m*
d-tehr-JEN-t

We have to clean up.	**Temos de fazer uma limpeza.**	TEH-moosh d fah-ZEHR OOH-mah leem-PEH-zah
The flat is already clean.	**A casa já está limpa.**	ah KAH-zah jah sh-TAH LEEM-pah
Who does the cleaning?	**Quem faz as limpezas?**	kain FAH-sh ash leem-PEH-zash?

LESSONS

 SCHOOL

white board
quadro branco
KWAH-drooh
BRAHN-kooh

chair
cadeira
kah-DAY-rah

book
livro
LEE-vrooh

table
mesa
MEH-zah

clock
relógio
rreh-LOH-jeeooh

teacher
professor
proh-feh-SOHR

student
estudante *m / f*
sh-tooh-DAHN-t

tablet
tablet
TAH-blet

calculator
máquina de calcular
MAH-kee-nah d kahl-kooh-LAHR

to go to school	**ir à escola**	eeh ah sh-KOH-lah	marks	**notas**	NOH-tash
to study	**estudar**	sh-tooh-DAHR	an oral exam	**um exame oral**	oohm eh-ZAH-m oh-RAHL
to learn	**aprender**	ah-prehn-DEHR	a written exam	**um exame escrito**	oohm eh-ZAH-m sh-KREE-tooh
to do homework	**fazer os trabalhos de casa**	fah-ZEHR oosh trah-BAH-lloosh d KAH-zah	to prepare for an exam	**preparar-se para um exame**	preh-pah-RAHR-s PAH-rah oohm eh-ZAH-m
to know	**saber**	sah-BEHR			
to take an exam	**fazer um exame**	fah-ZEHR oohm e-ZAH-m	to repeat a year	**repetir o ano**	rreh-p-TEEHR ooh AH-noh
to pass	**passar**	pah-SAHR			

Languages
Línguas
LEEN-gooh-ash

Spanish
Espanhol
sh-pah-NIOHL

German
Alemão
ah-I-MOAN

English
Inglês
een-GLEHSH

French
Francês
fran-SEHSH

Art
Educação visual *f*
eh-dooh-kah-SOAN
vee-zooh-AHL

Geography
Geografia
jee-ooh-grah-FEE-ah

Music
Educação musical *f*
eh-dooh-kah-SOAN mooh-
zee-KAHL

History
História
esh-TOH-ree-ah

Chemistry
Química
KEE-mee-kah

Biology
Biologia
Bee-ooh-looh-JEE-ah

Mathematics
Matemática
mah-t-MAH-tee-kah

Physical education
Educação física *f*
eh-dooh-kah-SOAN FEE-
zee-kah

scissors
tesoura
t-SOH-rah

globe
globo
GLOH-booh

school bag
mochila
moh-SHEE-lah

pen
caneta
kah-NEH-tah

notebook
caderno
kah-DEHR-nooh

pencil case
estojo
sh-TOH-jooh

ruler
régua
REH-gooah

pencil
lápis
LAH-peesh

pencil sharpener
afia lápis *m*
ah-FEE-ah LAH-peesh

rubber
borracha
booh-RRAH-shah

highlighter
marcador
mahr-kah-DOHR

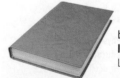

book
livro
LEE-vrooh

colouring pen
caneta de feltro
kah-NEH-tah d FEHL-trooh

stapler
agrafador
ah-grah-fah-DOHR

 WORK

job interview
entrevista de trabalho
en-tr-VEESH-tah d trah-BAH-llooh

recruiter
recrutador
reh-krooh-tah-DOHR

candidate
candidato
kahn-dee-DAH-tooh

application letter
carta de candidatura
KAHR-tah d kan-dee-dah-TOOH-rah

CV
CV
see-VEE

gross	**bruto**	BROOH-tooh		interview	**entrevista**	en-tr-VEESH-tah
net	**líquido**	LEE-kee-dooh		job	**trabalho**	trah-BAH-llooh
job advertisement	**anúncio de trabalho**	ah-NOON-see-ooh d trah-BAH-llooh		salary	**salário**	sah-LAH-ree-ooh
application	**candidatura**	kan-dee-dah-TOOH-rah		vacancy	**vaga**	VAH-gah
company	**empresa**	em-PREH-zah		work	**trabalho**	trah-BAH-llooh
education	**habilitações**	ah-bee-lee-tah-soansh		to hire	**contratar**	kon-trah-TAHR

experience	**experiência**	esh-peh-ree-EHN-see-ah
to apply for	**candidatar-se a**	kan-dee-dah-TAHR-s ah
assessment	**avaliação**	ah-vah-lee-ah-SOAN
bonus	**bónus**	BOH-noosh
employer	**empregador**	em-preh-gah-DOHR
to fire	**despedir**	dsh-p-DEER
fringe benefits	**benefícios adicionais**	beh-neh-FEE-see-oosh ah-dee-see-ooh-naish
maternity leave	**licença de maternidade**	lee-SEN-sah d mah-tehr-nee-DAH-d
notice	**notificação**	noh-tee-fee-kah-SOAN
staff	**pessoal**	p-sooh-AHL
human resource officer	**funcionário dos recursos humanos**	foon-see-ooh-NAH-ree-oosh doosh reh-KOOR-soosh ooh-MAH-noosh
promotion	**promoção**	proh-moh-SOAN
prospects	**perspetivas**	persh-peh-TEE-vash
to resign	**demitir-se**	deh-mee-TEER-s
to retire	**reformar-se**	rreh-foor-MAHR-s
sick leave	**baixa médica**	BAHI-shah MEH-dee-kah
strike	**greve**	GREH-v
trainee	**estagiário *m* / estagiária *f***	sh-tah-jee-AH-ree-ooh / sh-tah-jee-AH-ree-ah
training course	**curso de formação**	KOOR-sooh d foor-mah-SOAN
unemployment benefits	**subsídio de desemprego**	soob-SEE-dee-ooh d dez-em-PREH-gooh
workplace	**local de trabalho**	loo-KAHL d trah-BAH-llooh

employee
trabalhador
trah-bah-llah-DOHR

actor
ator *m* / **atriz** *f*
ah-TOH / ah-TREESH

baker
pasteleiro *m* /
pasteleira *f*
pash-t-LAY-rooh /
pash-t-LAY-rah

banker
banqueiro *m* /
banqueira *f*
ban-KAY-rooh /
ban-KAY-rah

butcher
talhante
tah-LLAN-t

carpenter
carpinteiro *m* /
carpinteira *f*
kahr-peen-TAY-rooh /
kahr-peen-TAY-rah

chef
cozinheiro *m* /
cozinheira *f*
koo-zee-NIAY-rooh /
koo-zee-NIAY-rah

doctor
médico *m* /
médica *f*
MEH-dee-kooh /
MEH-dee-kah

farmer
agricultor *m* /
agricultora *f*
ah-gree-kool-TOHR /
ah-gree-kool-TOH-rah

fisherman
pescador *m* /
pescadora *f*
psh-kah-DOHR / psh-
kah-DOH-rah

firefighter
bombeiro *m* /
bombeira *f*
bom-BAY-rooh /
bom-BAY-rah

musician
músico *m* /
música *f*
MOOH-zee-kooh /
MOOH-zee-kah

lawyer
advogado *m* /
advogada *f*
ad-vooh-GAH-
dooh / ad-vooh-
GAH-dah

nurse
enfermeiro *m* /
enfermeira *f*
en-fer-MAY-rooh /
en-fer-MAY-rah

pilot
piloto
pee-LOH-tooh

policeman
polícia
poh-LEE-see-ah

coach
treinador *m* /
treinadora *f*
tray-nah-DOHR /
tray-nah-DOH-rah

sailor
marinheiro *m* /
marinheira *f*
mah-ree-NIAY-rooh /
mah-ree-NIAY-rah

soldier
soldado
sohl-DAH-dooh

teacher
professor *m* /
professora *f*
pro-fe-SOR /
pro-fe-SO-rah

judge
juiz *m* /
juíza *f*
joo-EESH /
joo-EE-zah

tailor
alfaiate *m* /
costureira *f*
al-fay-AH-t /
koosh-tooh-
RAY-rah

veterinarian
veterinário *m* /
veterinária *f*
veh-teh-ree-NAH-ree-
ooh / veh-teh-ree-NAH-
ree-ah

waiter
empregado de mesa *m* /
empregada de mesa *f*
em-preh-GAH-dooh
d MEH-zah / em-preh-
GAH-dah d MEH-zah

mechanic
mecânico *m* /
mecânica *f*
meh-KAH-nee-kooh /
meh-KAH-nee-kah

accountant	**contabilista**	kon-tah-bee-LEESH-tah
barber	**barbeiro** *m* / **cabeleireira** *f*	bahr-BAY-rooh / kah-beh-lay-RAY-rah
beautician	**esteticista**	esh-teh-tee-SEESH-tah
broker	**corretor** *m* / **corretora** *f*	ko-rreh-TOHR / ko-rreh-TOH-rah
driver	**motorista**	moh-toh-REESH-tah
craftsman	**artesão** *m* / **artesã** *f*	ahr-t-SOAN / ahr-t-SAIN
dentist	**dentista**	den-TEESH-tah
engineer	**engenheiro** *m* / **engenheira** *f*	en-jeh-NIAY-rooh / en-jeh-NIAY-rah
pharmacist	**farmacêutico** *m* / **farmacêutica** *f*	fahr-mah-SEU-tee-kooh / fahr-mah-SEU-tee-kah
writer	**escritor** *m* / **escritora** *f*	sh-kree-TOHR / sh-kree-TOH-rah
politician	**político** *m* / **política** *f*	poh-LEE-tee-kooh / poh-LEE-tee-kah
professor	**professor** *m* / **professora** *f*	pro-fe-SOHR / pro-fe-SOH-rah
salesman	**vendedor** *m* / **vendedora** *f*	ven-deh-DOHR / ven-deh-DOH-rah
shoemaker	**sapateiro** *m* / **sapateira** *f*	sah-pah-TAY-rooh / sah-pah-TAY-rah
watchmaker	**relojoeiro** *m* / **relojoeira** *f*	rreh-looh-jooh-AY-rooh / rreh-looh-jooh-AY-rah
What's your occupation?	**Qual é a tua profissão?**	kwal eh ah tooah proh-fee-SOAN?
I work as a secretary.	**Eu sou secretária.**	ew soan seh-kreh-TAH-ree-ah
I am a teacher.	**Eu sou professor.**	ew soan pro-fe-SOHR

desk
secretária
seh-kreh-TAH-ree-ah

office
escritório
sh-kree-TOH-ree-ooh

computer
computador
kom-pooh-tah-DOHR

drawer
gaveta
gah-VEH-tah

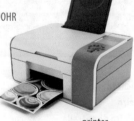

printer
impressora
eem-preh-SOH-rah

filing cabinet
arquivador
arh-kee-vah-DOHR

rubber stamp
carimbo
kah-REEM-booh

telephone
telefone *m*
t-l-FON

ink pad
almofada de tinta
ahl-mooh-FAH-dah d TEEN-tah

bin
caixote do lixo *m*
kai-SHOH-t dooh-LEE-shooh

swivel chair
cadeira giratória
ka-DAY-rah jee-rah-TOH-ree-ah

keyboard
teclado
teh-KLAH-dooh

clipboard	**prancheta**	pran-SHEH-tah
file	**ficheiro**	fee-SHAY-rooh
in-tray	**tabuleiro de entrada**	tah-boo-LAY-rooh d en-TRAH-dah
to photocopy	**fotocopiar**	foh-toh-kooh-pee-AHR
to print	**imprimir**	eem-pree-MEER

bulldog clip
mola para papel
MOH-lah PAH-rah
pah-PEHL

calculator
máquina de calcular
MAH-kee-nah d
kahl-kooh.LAHR

correction tape
corretor
kooh-rreh-TOHR

envelope
envelope *m*
en-v-LOH-p

laptop
computador portátil
kom-pooh-tah-DOHR pohr-TAH-teel

highlighter
marcador
mahr-kah-DOHR

letterhead
papel timbrado
pah-PEHL teem-BRAH-dooh

holepunch
furador
fooh-rah-DOHR

elastic bands
elásticos
ee-LASH-tee-koosh

notepad
bloco de notas
BLOH-kooh
d NOH-tash

pencil sharpener
afia lápis *m*
ah-FEE-ah LAH-peesh

paper clip
clip
kleep

personal organiser
agenda pessoal
ah-JEN-dah peh-sooh-AHL

pen
caneta
ka-NEH-tah

pencil
lápis
LAH-peesh

sticky tape
fita cola
FEE-tah KOH-lah

stapler
agrafador
ah-grah-fah-DOHR

staples
agrafos
ah-GRAH-foosh

 FOOD AND DRINK

apple juice
sumo de maçã
SOOH-mooh d
ma-SAIN

grapefruit juice
sumo de toranja
SOOH-mooh d tooh-
RAN-jah

orange juice
sumo de laranja
SOOH-mooh
d lah-RAN-jah

tomato juice
sumo de tomate
SOOH-mooh d tooh-
MAH-t

coffee
café *m*
kah-FEH

milk
leite *m*
LAY-t

tea
chá *m*
shah

with lemon
com limão
kom lee-MOAN

water
água
AH-gwah

with milk	**com leite**	kohn LAY-t	decaffeinated	**descafeinado**	dsh-kah-feh-ee-NAH-dooh
black	**preto**	PREH-tooh	fruit juice	**sumo de fruta**	SOOH-mooh d FROOH-tah

bacon
bacon
BAY-kon

banana
banana
bah-NAH-nah

berries
frutos do bosque
FROOH-toosh dooh BOSH-k

biscuit
bolacha
booh-LAH-shah

blueberries
mirtilo
meer-TEE-looh

bread
pão *m*
poan

jam
doce *m*
DOH-seh

butter
manteiga
mahn-TAY-gah

cereal
cereais *m*
seh-reh-AHEESH

cheese
queijo
KAY-jooh

cottage cheese
queijo fresco
KAY-jooh FRESH-kooh

doughnut
donut
DOH-noot

egg
ovo
OH-vooh

ham
fiambre *m*
fee-AM-br

honey
mel
mehl

marmalade
geleia
j-LAY-ah

omelette
omeleta
oh-meh-LEH-tah

pancake
crepe *m*
KREH-p

peanut butter
manteiga de amendoim
man-TAY-gah d ah-men-doh-EEM

sandwich
sanduíche *f*
sand-WEE-sh

sausage
salsicha
sal-SEE-shah

toast
torrada
tooh-RRAH-dah

waffle
waffle *f*
OOAH-fl

yoghurt
iogurte *m*
eeoh-GOOHR-t

breakfast
pequeno-almoço
pe-KEH-noog al-MOH-sooh

brunch
brunch
BRUN-sh

porridge
papas de aveia
PAH-pash d ah-VAY-ah

scrambled eggs
ovos mexidos
OH-voosh meh-SHEE-doosh

hard-boiled egg
ovo cozido
OH-vo kooh-ZEE-dooh

soft-boiled egg
ovo mal cozido
OH-vooh mahl kooh-ZEE-dooh

What do you eat for breakfast?	**O que tomas ao pequeno-almoço?**	ooh k TOH-mash ahoo pe-KEH-noog al-MOH-sooh?
When do you have breakfast?	**A que horas tomas o pequeno-almoço?**	ah k OH-rash TOH-mash ooh pe-KEH-noog al-MOH-sooh?
When does breakfast start?	**A que horas começa o pequeno-almoço?**	ah k OH-rash koo-MEH-sah ooh pe-KEH-noog al-MOH-sooh?
What would you like to drink?	**O que gostarias de beber?**	ooh k goosh-tah-REE-ash d beh-BEHR?
I would like a white tea.	**Queria um chá branco.**	keh-REE-ah oohm shah BRAN-kooh

bacon
bacon
BAY-kon

beef
carne de vaca *f*
KAHR-n d VAH-kah

chicken
frango
FRAN-gooh

duck
pato
PAH-tooh

ham
fiambre *m*
fee-AHM-br

kidneys
rins
reensh

lamb
borrego
boo-RREH-gooh

liver
fígado
fee-GAH-dooh

mince
carne picada *f*
KAHR-n pee-KAH-dah

pâté
paté *m*
pah-TEH

salami
salame *m*
sah-LAH-m

meat
carne *f*
KAHR-n

rabbit
coelho
kooh-AH-llooh

pork
carne de porco *f*
KAHR-n d POHR-kooh

sausage
salsicha
sal-SEE-shah

turkey
peru
peh-ROOH

veal
vitela
vee-TEH-lah

fruits
fruta
FROOH-tah

apple
maçã
mah-SAIN

apricot
alperce *m*
ahl-PEHR-s

banana
banana
bah-NAH-nah

blackberry
amora
ah-MOH-rah

blackcurrant
groselha-negra
groh-SAH-llah NEH-grah

blueberry
mirtilo
meer-TEE-looh

cherry
cerejas
seh-REH-jash

coconut
coco
KOH-kooh

fig
figo
FEE-gooh

grape
uvas
OOH-vash

grapefruit
toranja
tooh-RAN-jah

kiwi fruit
kiwi
kee-VEE

lemon
limão *m*
lee-MOAN

lime
lima
LEE-mah

mango
manga *m*
MAHN-gah

melon
melão
me-LOAN

orange
laranja
lah-RAHN-jah

peach
pêssego
PEH-seh-gooh

pear
pêra
PEH-rah

pineapple
ananás *m*
ah-nah-NASH

lychee
líchia
LEE-shee-ah

clementine
tangerina
tan-jeh-REE-nah

papaya
papaia
pah-PAY-ah

watermelon
melancia
meh-lan-SEE-ah

rhubarb
ruibarbo
rooy-BAHR-booh

kumqvat
kumquat
koom-KWAT

nectarine
nectarina
nek-tah-REE-nah

pomegranate
romã
rrooh-MAIN

raspberry
framboesa
frahm-booh-EH-zah

persimmon
dióspiro
dee-OH-sh-pee-rooh

strawberry
morango
moo-RAN-goo

plum
ameixa
ah-MAY-shah

redcurrant
groselha
groh-SAH-llah

passion fruit
maracujá *m*
mah-rah-kooh-JAH

vegetables
legumes *m*
leh-GOO-msh

artichoke
alcachofra
ahl-kah-SHOH-frah

asparagus
espargos
sh-PAHR-goosh

avocado
abacate *m*
ah-bah-KAT

beansprouts
rebentos de feijão
rreh-BEHN-toosh d fay-JOAN

beetroot
beterraba
beh-teh-RRAH-bah

broccoli
brócolos
BROH-kooh-loosh

brussels sprouts
couves de Bruxelas *f*
KAU-vsh d broo-SHEH-lash

cabbage
couve *f*
KAU-v

aubergine
beringela
beh-reen-JEH-lah

carrot
cenoura
seh-NOH-rah

cauliflower
couve-flor *f*
KAU-v flohr

celery
aipo
AEE-pooh

courgette
courgette *f*
koor-JET

cucumber
pepino
peh-PEE-nooh

garlic
alho
AH-llooh

ginger
gengibre *m*
jen-JEE-br

leek
alho francês
AH-llo fran-SESH

lettuce
alface *f*
ahl-FAH-s

mushroom
cogumelo
kooh-gooh-MEH-looh

onion
cebola
seh-BOH-lah

peas
ervilhas
eer-VEE-llash

potato
batata
bah-TAH-tah

pumpkin
abóbora
ah-BOH-booh-rah

spinach
espinafres *m*
sh-pee-NAH-fresh

radish
rabanete *m*
rrah-bah-NET

sweetcorn
milho
MEE-llooh

tomato
tomate *m*
tooh-MAH-t

spring onion
cebolinho
seh-booh-LEE-nioo

red pepper
pimento vermelho
pee-MEN-tooh ver-MAH-llooh

green beans
feijão verde *m*
fay-JOAN VER-d

chicory
chicória
shee-KOOH-ree-ah

turnip
nabo
NAH-booh

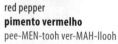

cuttlefish
choco
SHOH-kooh

haddock
hadoque *m*
ah-DOH-k

lemon sole
solha-limão
SOH-llah lee-MOAN

halibut
alabote *m*
ah-lah-BOH-t

mackerel
cavala
kah-VAH-lah

monkfish
tamboril
tam-booh-reel

mussels
mexilhões *m*
meh-shee-LLOINS

sardine
sardinha
sahr-DEE-niah

sea bass
robalo
rooh-BAH-looh

sea bream
dourada
doh-RAH-dah

swordfish
peixe espada *m*
PAY-sh sh-PAH-dah

trout
truta
TROOH-tah

crab
caranquejo
kah-rahn-GAY-jooh

crayfish
lagostim
lah-goosh-TEEM

lobster
lagosta
lah-GOSH-tah

tuna
atum
AH-toom

octopus
polvo
POHL-vooh

oyster
ostra
OSH-trah

prawn / shrimp
camarão
kah-mah-ROAN

scallop
vieira
vee-AY-rah

salmon
salmão
sal-MOAN

squid
lula
LOOH-lah

fish	**peixe** *m*	PAY-sh
cleaned	**limpo**	LEEM-pooh
fresh	**fresco**	FRESH-kooh
frozen	**congelado**	kon-jeh-LAH-dooh
salted	**salgado**	sahl-GAH-dooh
skinned	**sem pele**	sain PEH-l
smoked	**fumado**	foo-mah-dooh

cheese
queijo
KAY-jooh

cream
natas
NAH-tash

egg
ovo
OH-vooh

milk
leite *m*
LAY-t

cottage cheese
queijo fresco
KAY-jooh FRESH-kooh

blue cheese
queijo azul
KAY-joo ah-ZOOL

butter
manteiga
mahn-TAY-gah

goat's cheese	**queijo de cabra**	KAY-jooh d KAH-brah	skimmed milk	**leite magro** *m*	LAY-t MAH-grooh
margarine	**margarina**	mahr-gah-REE-nah	sour cream	**natas azedas**	NAH-tash ah-ZEH-dash
full-fat milk	**leite gordo** *m*	LAY-t GOHR-dooh	yoghurt	**iogurte**	ioh-GOOH-rt
semi-skimmed milk	**leite meio gordo** *m*	LAY-t MAY-oog GOHR-dooh	crème fraîche	**crème fraîche** *m*	krehm FRAY-sh

baguette
baguete *f*
bah-GEH-t

bread rolls
pãezinhos *m*
pain-ZEE-nioosh

brown bread
pão escuro *m*
poan sh-KOOH-rooh

cake
bolo
BOH-looh

loaf
pão *m*
poan

white bread
pão branco *m*
poan BRAHN-kooh

garlic bread	**pão de alho** *m*	poan d AH-llooh	quiche	**quiche** *f*	KEE-sh
pastry	**pastelaria**	pash-t-lah-REE-ah	sliced loaf	**pão de forma** *m*	poan d FOHR-mah
pitta bread	**pão pita** *m*	poan PEE-tah	sponge cake	**pão-de-ló** *m*	poan d loh

FOOD AND DRINK 6.9 CONDIMENTS, SAUCES AND HERBS

ketchup	mayonnaise	mustard	vinegar	salt	pepper
ketchup	**maionese** *f*	**mostarda**	**vinagre** *m*	**sal**	**pimenta**
ket-SHAP	mai-o-NEH-s	moosh-TAHR-dah	vee-NAH-gr	sal	pee-MEN-tah

basil	**manjericão** *m*	man-jehr-ee-KOAN		paprika	**colorau**	koh-loh-ROW
chilli powder	**malagueta em pó**	mah-lah-GEH-tah em poh		parsley	**salsa**	SAHL-sah
chives	**cebolinho**	seh-boh-LEE-niooh		rosemary	**alecrim**	ah-leh-KREEM
cinnamon	**canela**	kah-NEH-lah		saffron	**açafrão**	ah-sah-FROAN
coriander	**coentros**	kooh-EHN-troosh		sage	**salva**	SAHL-vah
cumin	**cominho**	kooh-MEE-niooh		salad dressing	**molho para salada**	MOH-llooh PAH-rah sah-LAH-dah
curry	**caril**	kah-REEL		spices	**especiarias**	esh-pe-see-ah-REE-ash
dill	**endro**	EN-drooh		thyme	**tomilho**	tooh-MEE-llooh
nutmeg	**noz moscada** *m*	nosh moosh-KAH-dah		vinaigrette	**vinagrete**	vee-nah-GREH-t

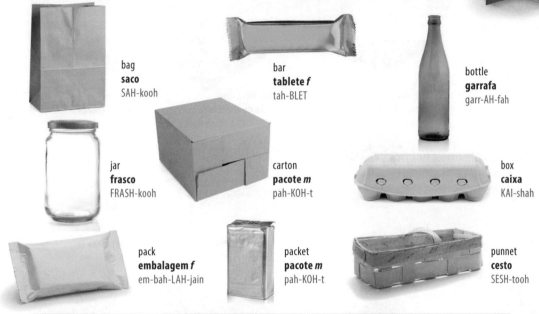

bag
saco
SAH-kooh

bar
tablete *f*
tah-BLET

bottle
garrafa
garr-AH-fah

jar
frasco
FRASH-kooh

carton
pacote *m*
pah-KOH-t

box
caixa
KAI-shah

pack
embalagem *f*
em-bah-LAH-jain

packet
pacote *m*
pah-KOH-t

punnet
cesto
SESH-tooh

a bag of potatoes	**um saco de batatas**	oohm SAH-kooh d bah-TAH-tash
chocolate bar	**tablete de chocolate** *f*	tah-BLET d shooh-kooh-LAT
two bottles of mineral water	**duas garrafas de água mineral**	DOO-ash gah-RRAH-fash d AH-gwah mee-neh-RAHL
a carton of milk	**um pacote de leite**	oohm pah-KOT d LAY-t
a jar of jam	**um frasco de doce**	oohm FRASH-kooh d DOH-s

biscuit
bolacha
booh-LAH-shah

chocolate
chocolate *m*
shooh-kooh-LAT

chocolate cake
bolo de chocolate
BOH-looh d shooh-kooh-LAT

apple pie
tarte de maçã *f*
TAHR-t d ma-SAIN

doughnut
donut
DOH-noot

fruit cake
bolo de fruta
BOH-looh d FROOH-tah

fruit salad
salada de fruta
sah-LAH-dah d FROOH-tah

cheesecake
cheesecake *m*
cheese-cake

gingerbread
bolacha de gengibre
boo-LAH-shah d jen-JEE-br

ice cream
gelado
jeh-LAH-dooh

muffin
queque *m*
KEH-k

chocolate mousse
mousse de chocolate *f*
moose d shooh-kooh-LAT

milkshake
batido
bah-TEE-dooh

marshmallow
marshmallow *m*
marsh-MAH-low

macaroon
macarron
mah-kah-RROHN

waffle
waffle *f*
WAH-ffle

pancakes
crepes *m*
KREH-psh

strudel
folhado
foo-LLAH-dooh

pudding
pudim *m*
poo-DEEM

honey
mel
mehl

cake	**bolo**	BOH-looh
coconut cake	**bolo de coco**	BOH-looh d KOH-kooh
dessert	**sobremesa**	soh-br-MEH-zah
frozen yoghurt	**iogurte gelado** *m*	io-GOOH-rt jeh-LAH-dooh
rice pudding	**arroz doce**	ah-RROSH DOH-s
I like to eat sweets.	**Gosto de comer doces.**	GOSH-tooh d kooh-MEHR DOH-sesh
I cannot eat anything sweet.	**Não consigo comer nada doce.**	noan kon-SEE-gooh kooh-MEHR NAH-dah DOH-s

cheeseburger
hambúrguer com queijo
am-BOOR-gehr kom KAY-jooh

hot dog
cachorro quente
kah-SHOH-rrooh KEN-t

fish sandwich
sandes de peixe *f*
SAN-dsh d PAY-sh

fried chicken
frango frito
FRAN-gooh FREE-tooh

French fries
batatas fritas
bah-TAH-tash FREE-tash

nachos
nachos
NAH-shoosh

taco
taco
TAH-kooh

burrito
burrito
booh-REE-tooh

pizza
pizza
PEE-zah

hamburger
hambúrguer
am-BOOR-gher

chicken sandwich
sandes de frango *f*
SAN-dsh d FRAN-gooh

fish and chips
peixe e batatas fritas *m*
PAY-sh ee bah-TAH-tash FREE-tash

to peel	**descascar**	desh-kash-KAHR
to grate	**ralar**	rah-LAHR
to chop	**picar**	pee-KAHR
to crush	**esmagar**	shmah-GARH
to beat	**bater**	bah-TEHR
to grease	**untar**	oon-TAHR
to break	**partir**	pahr-TEER
to stir	**misturar**	meesh-tooh-RAHR
to knead	**amassar**	ah-mah-SAHR
to steam	**cozinhar a vapor**	kooh-zee-NIAHR ah vah-POHR
to weigh	**pesar**	peh-ZAHR
to add	**adicionar**	ah-dee-see-ooh-NAHR
to bake	**assar**	ah-SAHR
to stir-fry	**refogar**	reh-fooh-GAHR
to grill	**grelhar**	greh-LLAHR
to roast	**tostar**	toosh-TAHR
to barbecue	**fazer um churrasco**	fah-ZEHR oohm shooh-RRASH-kooh
to fry	**fritar**	free-TAHR

to wash
lavar
lah-VAHR

to cut
cortar
koor-TAHR

to mix
misturar
meesh-tooh-RAHR

to boil
ferver
fer-VEHR

bar
balcão
bahl-KOAN

buffet
buffet
booh-FEH

bill
conta
KON-tah

bistro
bistrô
bees-TROH

café
café *m*
kah-FEH

dessert
sobremesa
soh-breh-MEH-zah

menu
menu
meh-NOOH

canteen
cantina
kan-TEE-nah

pizzeria
pizzaria
pee-zah-REE-ah

pub
bar
bahr

salad bar
buffet de saladas
booh-FEH d sah-LAH-dahsh

deli
delicatesse *f*
deh-lee-kah-TEH-s

self-service
self-service
self SER-vis

take-out / take-away
para levar
PAH-rah leh-VAHR

waiter
empregado de mesa
em-preh-GAH-dooh d MEH-zah

waitress
empregada de mesa
em-preh-GAH-dah d MEH-zah

à la carte	**à la carte**	ah lah KAHR-t
starter	**entrada**	en-TRAH-dah
booking	**reservar**	rreh-ser-VAHR
complimentary	**gratuito**	grah-TOOEE-tooh
dish	**prato**	PRAH-tooh
main course	**prato principal**	PRAH-too preen-see-PAHL
to order	**pedir**	peh-DEER
speciality	**especialidade**	esh-peh-see-ah-lee-DAH-d
aperitif	**aperitivo**	ah-pe-ree-TEE-vooh

What do you want to order?	**O que vai pedir?**	oo k vaee p-DEER
I would like to see the menu.	**Gostaria de ver o menu.**	goosh-tah-REE-ah d vehr ooh meh-NOOH
We'll take the set menu.	**Queremos o menu do dia.**	ke-REH-moosh ooh meh-NOOH dooh deeah

TRAVEL AND LEISURE

to travel by bus
viajar de autocarro
viah-JAHR d aw-toh-KAH-rrooh

to travel by plane
viajar de avião
viah-JAHR d ah-vee-OAN

to travel by car
viajar de carro
viah-JAHR d KAH-rrooh

to travel by bicycle
viajar de bicicleta
viah-JAHR d bee-see-KLEH-tah

to travel by motorcycle
viajar de mota
viah-JAHR d MOH-tah

travel agency
agência de viagens
ah-JEN-see-ah d vee-AH-jensh

family holiday
férias em família
FEH-ree-ash ain fah-MEE-lee-ah

safari
safari
sah-FAH-ree

honeymoon
lua-de-mel
looah d mehl

beach holiday
férias na praia
FEH-ree-ash nah PRAEE-ah

round-the-world trip
viagem à volta do mundo *f*
vee-AH-jain ah VOHL-tah dooh
MOON-dooh

cruise
cruzeiro
krooh-ZAY-rooh

to book
reservar
reh-zer-VAHR

long-haul destination
destino de longo curso
desh-TEE-nooh d LON-gooh
KOOR-sooh

guided tour
visita guiada
vee-ZEE-tah ghee-AH-dah

out of season
fora de época
FOH-rah d EH-pooh-kah

picturesque village
vila pitoresca
VEE-lah pee-tooh-RESH-kah

landscape
paisagem *f*
pah-ee-ZAH-jain

to go sightseeing
fazer turismo
fah-ZEHR tooh-REESH-mooh

city break
escapadinha a uma cidade
esh-kah-pah-DEE-niah ah
OOH-mah see-DAH-d

holiday brochure	**folheto de férias**	foo-LLEH-tooh d FEH-ree-ash
holiday destination	**destino de férias**	desh-TEE-nooh d FEH-ree-ash
package tour	**pacote turístico** *m*	pah-KOT tooh-REESH-tee-koo
places of interest	**locais de interesse**	loo-KAISH d een-t-REH-ss
short break	**escapadinha**	esh-kah-pah-DEE-niah
tourist attractions	**atrações turísticas** *f*	ah-trah-SOIN-sh tooh-REESH-tee-kash
tourist trap	**armadilha para turistas**	ahr-mah-DEE-llah PAH-rah tooh-REESH-tash

Afghanistan
Afganistão *m*
ahf-gah-neesh-TOAN

Angola
Angola
ahn-GOH-lah

Aruba
Aruba
ah-ROOH-bah

The Bahamas
Baamas
bah-AH-mash

Belarus
Bielorrússia
bee-eh-loh-RROOH-see-ah

Albania
Albânia
ahl-BAH-nee-ah

Antigua and Barbuda
Antigua e Barbuda
ahn-TEE-gwa ee bar-BOOH-dah

Australia
Austrália
ahoosh-TRAH-lee-ah

Bahrain
Bahrain
bah-RAHIN

Belgium
Bélgica
behl-JEE-kah

Algeria
Algéria
ahl-JEH-ree-ah

Argentina
Argentina
ahr-jen-TEE-nah

Austria
Áustria
AHOOSH-tree-ah

Bangladesh
Bangladesh
bang-lah-DESH

Belize
Belize *m*
beh-LEE-z

Andorra
Andorra
ahn-DOH-rrah

Armenia
Arménia
ahr-MEH-nee-ah

Azerbaijan
Azerbaijão
azehr-bay-JOAN

Barbados
Barbados
bahr-BAH-doosh

Benin
Benim *m*
beh-NEEM

Bhutan
Butão *m*
booh-TOAN

Brazil
Brasil
brah-ZEEL

Burma
Birmânia
beer-MAH-nee-ah

Canada
Canadá *m*
kah-nah-DAH

Chile
Chile *m*
SHEE-I

Bolivia
Bolívia
boh-LEE-vee-ah

Brunei
Brunei
brooh-NAY

Burundi
Burundi
booh-ROON-dee

Cape Verde
Cabo Verde
KAH-booh VER-d

China
China
SHEE-nah

Bosnia and Herzegovina
Bósnia e Herzegovina
BOHSH-nee-ah ee ehr-zeh-goh-VEE-nah

Bulgaria
Bulgária
boohl-GAH-ree-ah

Cambodia
Cambodja *m*
kam-BOH-djah

Central African Republic
República Centro-Africana
reh-POOH-blee-kah SEN-trooh ah-free-KAH-nah

Colombia
Colômbia
kooh-LOM-bee-ah

Botswana
Botswana *m*
bohtz-WAH-nah

Burkina Faso
Burkina Faso *m*
boohr-KEE-nah FAH-zooh

Cameroon
Camarões *m*
kah-mah-ROINSH

Chad
Chad
shad

Comoros
Comores
koh-MOH-resh

Democratic Republic
of the Congo
**República Democrática
do Congo**
reh-POOH-blee-kah deh-moh
-KRAH-tee-kah dooh KON-gooh

Republic of the Congo
República do Congo
reh-POOH-blee-kah dooh KON-
gooh

Costa Rica
Costa Rica
KOSH-tah REE-kah

Côte d'Ivoire
Costa do Marfim
KOSH-tah dooh mahr-FEEM

Croatia
Croácia
krooh-AH-see-ah

Cuba
Cuba
KOOH-bah

Curacao
Curaçao
kooh-rah-SAO

Cyprus
Chipre *m*
SHEE-pr

Czechia
República Checa
Reh-POOH-blee-kah SHEH-kah

Denmark
Dinamarca
dee-nah-MAHR-kah

Djibouti
Djibouti
djee-booh-TEE

Dominica
Dominica
doh-mee-NEE-kah

Dominican Republic
República Dominicana
reh-POOH-blee-kah dooh-mee-
nee-KAH-nah

East Timor
Timor Leste
tee-MOHR LESH-t

Ecuador
Equador
eh-kwah-DOHR

Egypt
Egito
eh-JEE-tooh

El Salvador
El Salvador
ehl sahl-vah-DOHR

Equatorial Guinea
Guiné Equatorial
ghee-NEH eh-kwa-
toh-ree-AHL

Eritrea
Eritreia
eh-ree-TRAY-ah

Estonia
Estónia
esh-TOH-nee-ah

France
França
FRAN-sah

Germany
Alemanha
ah-leh-MAH-nia

Guatemala
Guatemala
gwa-t-MAH-lah

Haiti
Haiti
ahee-TEE

Ethiopia
Etiópia
eh-tee-OH-pee-ah

Gabon
Gabão *m*
gah-BOAN

Ghana
Gana
GAH-nah

Guinea
Guiné *m*
ghee-NEH

Honduras
Honduras
on-DOOH-rash

Fiji
Fiji
FEE-jee

The Gambia
Gâmbia
GAM-bee-ah

Greece
Grécia
GREH-see-ah

Guinea-Bissau
Guiné Bissau *f*
ghee-NEH bee-SAOOH

Hong Kong
Hong Kong
OHN-g KOHN-g

Finland
Finlândia
feen-LAHN-dee-ah

Georgia
Geórgia
jeh-OHR-jee-ah

Grenada
Granada
grah-NAH-dah

Guyana
Guiana
ghee-AH-nah

Hungary
Hungria
oohn-GREE-ah

Iceland
Islândia
eesh-LAN-dee-ah

Iraq
Iraque *m*
ee-RAK

Jamaica
Jamaica
jah-MAEE-kah

Kenya
Quénia *m*
KEH-nee-ah

Kosovo
Kosovo
Koh-ZOH-vooh

India
Índia
een-DEE-ah

Ireland
Irlanda
eer-LAHN-dah

Japan
Japão
jah-poan

Kiribati
Kiribati
Kee-ree-bah-tee

Kuwait
Kuwait
kooh-AIT

Indonesia
Indonésia
een-doh-NEH-zee-ah

Israel
Israel
Eesh-RAH-ehl

Jordan
Jordânia
johr-DAH-nee-ah

North Korea
Coreia do Norte
koo-RAY-ah dooh NOHR-t

Kyrgyzstan
Quirguistão *m*
keer-gheesh-TOAN

Iran
Irão
ee-roan

Italy
Itália
ee-TAH-lee-ah

Kazakhstan
Cazaquistão *m*
kah-zah-keesh-toan

South Korea
Coreia do Sul
koo-RAY-ah dooh sool

Laos
Laos
LAH-os

Latvia
Letónia
leh-TOH-nee-ah

Libya
Líbia
LEE-bee-ah

Macau
Macau
mah-KAOOH

Malaysia
Malásia
mah-LAH-zee-ah

Marshall Islands
Ilhas Marshall
EE-llash MAHR-shal

Lebanon
Líbano
LEE-bah-nooh

Liechtenstein
Liechtenstein
Leesh-tehn-stahin

Macedonia
Macedónia
mah-seh-DOH-nee-ah

Maldives
Maldivas
mahl-DEE-vash

Mauritania
Mauritânia
maooh-ree-TAH-nee-ah

Lesotho
Lesoto
leh-ZOH-tooh

Lithuania
Lituânia
Lee-tooh-AH-nee-ah

Madagascar
Madagáscar
Mah-dah-GASH-kahr

Mali
Mali
Mah-LEE

Mauritius
Ilhas Maurícias
EE-llash maooh-REE-see-ash

Liberia
Libéria
lee-BEH-ree-ah

Luxembourg
Luxemburgo
Loosh-em-BOOR-ghooh

Malawi
Malawi
mah-lah-WEE

Malta
Malta
MAHL-tah

Mexico
México
MEH-shee-kooh

Micronesia
Micronésia
mee-krooh-NEH-zee-ah

Montenegro
Montenegro
mohn-t-NEH-grooh

Nauru
Nauru
nah-ooh-ROOH

Nicaragua
Nicarágua
nee-ka-RAH-goo-ah

Oman
Omã *m*
oh-MAIN

Moldova
Moldávia
mohl-DAH-vee-ah

Morocco
Marrocos
mah-RROH-koosh

Nepal
Nepal
neh-PAHL

Niger
Níger
NEE-jehr

Pakistan
Paquistão
Pah-keesh-toan

Monaco
Mónaco
MOH-nah-kooh

Mozambique
Moçambique
mooh-sam-BEE-k

Netherlands
Holanda
oh-LAHN-dah

Nigeria
Nigéria
nee-JEH-ree-ah

Palau
Palau
pah-LAOOH

Mongolia
Mongólia
mohn-GOH-lee-ah

Namibia
Namíbia
nah-MEE-bee-ah

New Zealand
Nova Zelândia
NOH-vah z-LAHN-dee-ah

Norway
Noruega
noh-rooh-EH-gah

Palestinian Territories
Territórios Palestinianos
teh-rreeh-TOH-ree-oosh
pah-lesh-tee-nee-AH-noosh

Panama
Panamá
pah-nah-MAH

Peru
Peru
peh-ROOH

Qatar
Qatar
kah-TAHR

Saint Lucia
Santa Lúcia
SAN-tah LOOH-see-ah

Senegal
Senegal
seh-neh-GAHL

Papua New Guinea
Papua Nova Guiné
pah-POOH-ah NOH-vah
gheen-NEH

Philippines
Filipinas
fee-lee-PEE-nash

Romania
Roménia
rrooh-MEH-nee-ah

Samoa
Samoa
sah-MOH-ah

Serbia
Sérvia
SEHR-vee-ah

Paraguay
Paraguai
pah-rah-GWAH-ee

Poland
Polónia
pooh-LOH-nee-ah

Russia
Rússia
rrOOH-see-ah

San Marino
São Marino
soan mah-REE-nooh

Seychelles
Seicheles
say-SHEH-lsh

Portugal
Portugal
poohr-tooh-GAHL

Rwanda
Ruanda
rrooh-AHN-dah

Saudi Arabia
Arábia Saudita
ah-RAH-bee-ah saooh-
DEE-tah

Sierra Leone
Serra Leoa
SEH-rrah lee-OH-ah

Singapore
Singapura
seen-gah-POOH-rah

Solomon Islands
Ilhas Solomon
EE-llash soh-loh-MOHN

Sri Lanka
Sri Lanka
sree LAHN-kah

Swaziland
Suazilândia
swah-zee-LAHN-dee-ah

Taiwan
Taiwan
Tai-wahn

Sint Maarten
Sint Maarten
seent MAHR-tehn

Somalia
Somália
soh-MAH-lee-ah

Sudan
Sudão *m*
sooh-DOAN

Sweden
Suécia
sooh-EH-see-ah

Tajikistan
Tajiquistão *m*
tah-jee-keesh-TOAN

Slovakia
Eslováquia
esh-loh-VAH-kee-ah

South Africa
África do Sul
AH-free-kah dooh soohl

South Sudan
Sudão do Sul *m*
sooh-DOAN dooh soohl

Switzerland
Suíça
SWEE-sah

Tanzania
Tanzânia
tahn-ZAH-nee-ah

Slovenia
Eslovénia
esh-loh-VEH-nee-ah

Spain
Espanha
esh-PAH-niah

Suriname
Suriname *m*
sooh-ree-NAHM-m

Syria
Síria
SEE-ree-ah

Thailand
Tailândia
tai-LAHN-dee-ah

Togo
Togo
TOH-goh

Turkey
Turquia
toor-KEE-ah

Ukraine
Ucrânia
ooh-KRAH-nee-ah

Uruguay
Uruguai
Ooh-roo-gwahee

Vietnam
Vietnam
vee-eht-NAHM

Tonga
Tonga *m*
TOHN-gah

Turkmenistan
Turquemenistão *m*
toor-k-mehn-eesh-TOAN

United Arab Emirates
Emiratos Árabes Unidos
eh-mee-RAH-toosh AH-rah-bsh
ooh-NEE-doosh

Uzbekistan
Uzebequistão *m*
ooh-zeh-beh-keesh-TOAN

Yemen
Iémen
ee-EH-mehn

Trinidad and Tobago
Trinidad e Tobago
tree-nee-DAh-d ee
tooh-BAH-gooh

Tuvalu
Tuvalu
tooh-VAH-looh

United Kingdom
Reino Unido
RAY-nooh ooh-NEE-dooh

Vanuatu
Vanuatu
vah-nooh-AH-tooh

Zambia
Zâmbia
ZAHM-bee-ah

Tunisia
Tunísia
tooh-NEE-zee-ah

Uganda
Uganda *m*
ooh-GHAN-dah

United States of America
Estados Unidos da América
esh-TAH-doosh ooh-NEE-
doosh dah ah-MEH-ree-kah

Venezuela
Venezuela
veh-neh-zooh-EH-lah

Zimbabwe
Zimbabué *m*
zeem-bah-booh-EH

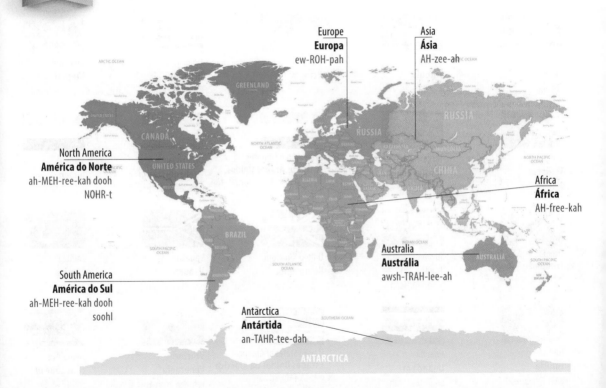

Europe
Europa
ew-ROH-pah

Asia
Ásia
AH-zee-ah

North America
América do Norte
ah-MEH-ree-kah dooh
NOHR-t

Africa
África
AH-free-kah

South America
América do Sul
ah-MEH-ree-kah dooh
soohl

Australia
Austrália
awsh-TRAH-lee-ah

Antarctica
Antártida
an-TAHR-tee-dah

bus stop
paragem de autocarro *f*
pah-RAH-jain d aw-toh-KAH-rrooh

platform
plataforma
plah-tah-FOHR-mah

(aero)plane
avião *m*
ah-vee-OAN

moped / scooter
scooter *f*
SKOOH-tehr

(bi)cycle
bicicleta
bee-see-KLEH-tah

boat
barco
BAHR-kooh

bus
autocarro
aw-toh-KAH-rroh

ship
navio
nah-VEEOOH

car
carro
KAH-rroh

helicopter
helicóptero
eh-lee-KOH-pt-rooh

lorry
camião *m*
kah-mee-oan

tanker
petroleiro
peh-troh-LAY-rooh

kid's scooter
trotineta
troh-tee-NEH-tah

(motor)bike
moto f
MOH-toh

train
comboio
kom-BOY-ooh

taxi
táxi
TAH-ksee

ferry
ferry
FEH-rree

submarine
submarino
soob-mah-REE-nooh

sailing boat
barco à vela
BAHR-kooh ah VEH-lah

tram
elétrico
ee-LEH-tree-kooh

by air	**de avião**	d ah-vee-OAN		in the port	**no porto**	nooh POHR-tooh
on the motorway	**na autoestrada**	nah aw-toh-sh-TRAH-dah		by rail	**de comboio**	d kom-BOY-ooh
on the road	**na estrada**	nah sh-TRAH-dah		by tube / underground	**de metro**	d MEH-trooh
by sea	**de barco**	d BAHR-kooh		on foot	**a pé**	on foot

airport
aeroporto
ah-eh-roh-POHR-tooh

arrivals
chegadas
sheh-GAH-dash

departures
partidas
pahr-TEE-dash

luggage
bagagem *f*
bah-GAH-jain

carry-on luggage
bagagem de mão *f*
bah-GAH-jain d moan

oversized baggage
bagagem fora do formato *f*
bah-GAH-jain FOH-rah dooh foor-MAH-tooh

check-in desk
balcão de check-in *m*
bal-KOAN d check-in

customs
alfândega
ahl-FAHN-d-gah

baggage reclaim
recolha de bagagem
rreh-KOH-llah d bah-GAH-jain

boarding pass
cartão de embarque *m*
kahr-TOAN d emb-ARH-k

flight ticket
bilhete de avião *m*
bee-LLET d ah-vee-OAN

economy class
classe turística *f*
KLAH-s too-REESH-tee-kah

business class
primeira classe
pree-MAY-rah KLAH-s

arrivals lounge
chegadas
she-GAH-dash

delayed
atrasado
ah-trah-ZAH-dooh

to board a plane
embarcar num avião
em-bahr-KAHR noom ah-vee-OAN

gate
porta de embarque
POHR-tah d emb-AHR-k

passport
passaporte *m*
pah-sah-POHR-t

passport control
controlo de passaportes
kon-TROH-looh d pah-sah-POHR-t

security check
controlo de segurança
kon-TROH-looh d seh-gooh-RAN-sah

airline	**linha aérea**	LEE-niah ah-EH-reah	long-haul flight	**voo de longo curso**	VOH-ooh d LON-gooh KOOR-sooh
boarding time	**hora de embarque**	OH-rah d emb-AHR-k			
charter flight	**voo charter**	VOH-ooh SHAHR-tehr	The flight has been delayed.	**O voo está atrasado.**	ooh VOH-ooh shtah ah-trah-ZAH-dooh
on time	**a horas**	ah OH-rash			
one-way ticket	**bilhete de ida** *m*	bee-LLET d EE-dah	to book a ticket to...	**comprar um bilhete para...**	kohmp-RAHR oohm bee-LLET PAH-rah...
return ticket	**bilhete de ida e volta** *m*	bee-LLET d EE-dah ee VOHL-tah			

railway station
estação de caminhos-de-ferro f
esh-ta-soan d kah-MEE-niosh d FEH-rrooh

train
comboio
kom-BOY-ooh

platform
plataforma
plah-tah-FOHR-mah

express train	comboio rápido	kom-BOY-ooh RRAH-pee-dooh
to get on the train	embarcar no comboio	em-bahr-KAHR nooh- kom-BOY-ooh
to get off the train	sair do comboio	sah-EER dooh- kom-BOY-ooh
to miss a train	perder um comboio	pehr-DEHR oohm kom-BOY-ooh

train driver
motorista de comboio *m*
mooh-tooh-REESH-tah d
kom-BOY-ooh

travelcard
cartão de viagem *m*
kar-TOAN d vee-AH-jain

train journey
viagem de comboio *f*
vee-AH-jain d kom-BOY-ooh

carriage
carruagem *f*
kah-rrooh-AH-jain

seat
lugar
loo-gahr

station
estação *f*
esh-tah-SOAN

restaurant car
vagão restaurante *m*
vah-GOAN resh-TAHW-rahn-t

sleeper train
comboio-hotel
kom-BOY-ooh oh-TEHL

toilet
casa de banho
KAH-zah d BAH-nioo

coach
autocarro
aw-toh-KAH-rroosh

bus driver
motorista de autocarro *m*
mooh-tooh-REESH-tah d
aw-toh-KAH-rrooh

bus stop
paragem de autocarro *f*
pah-RAH-jain d aw-toh-KAH-rrooh

validator
validador
vah-lee-dah-DOHR

double-decker bus
autocarro de dois andares
aw-toh-KAH-rrooh d doish
ahn-DAH-rsh

bus journey
viagem de autocarro *f*
vee-AH-jain d aw-toh-KAH-rrooh

coach station
terminal de autocarros
tehr-mee-NAHL d aw-toh-KAH-
rroosh

request stop
pedir para parar
peh-DEER PAH-rah pah-
RAHR

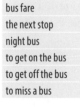

bus fare	**bilhete de autocarro** *m*	bee-LLET d aw-toh-KAH-rrooh
the next stop	**a próxima paragem**	ah PROH-see-mah pah-RAH-jain
night bus	**autocarro noturno**	aw-toh-KAH-rrooh noh-TOOR-nooh
to get on the bus	**entrar no autocarro**	ehn-TRAHR nooh aw-toh-KAH-rrooh
to get off the bus	**sair do autocarro**	sah-EER dooh aw-toh-KAH-rrooh
to miss a bus	**perder um autocarro**	pehr-DEHR oohm aw-toh-KAH-rrooh

hotel
hotel
oh-TEHL

campsite
zona de acampamento
ZOH-nah d ah-kahm-pah-
MEN-tooh

holiday resort
estância de férias
esh-TANH-see-a d FEH-
ree-ash

youth hostel
pousada da juventude
poh-ZAH-dah dah
jooh-vehn-TOOH-d

accommodation	**alojamento**	ah-looh-jah-MEHN-tooh
all-inclusive	**tudo incluído**	TOOH-dooh een-klooh-EE-dooh
half-board	**meia pensão** *f*	MAY-ah pehn-SOAN
full-board	**pensão completa** *f*	pehn-SOAN kom-PLEH-tah
self-catering	**com cozinha**	kom koo-ZEE-niah
Can you recommend a hotel?	**Podes recomendar-me um hotel?**	POH-dsh reh-kooh-mehn-DAHR-m oohm oh-TEHL?
We are staying at the hotel "XZ".	**Estamos alojados no hotel "XZ".**	esh-TAH-moosh ah-looh-JAH-doosh nooh oh-TEHL "XZ"
Have you already booked the hotel?	**Já reservaste o hotel?**	jah reh-zehr-VASH-t ooh oh-TEHL?
I'm looking for a place to stay.	**Estou à procura de alojamento.**	esh-TOU ah proh-KOO-rah d ah-looh-jah-MEHN-tooh

bed and breakfast
alojamento e pequeno-almoço
ah-loo-jah-MEN-tooh ee peh-
KEH-noo ahl-MOH-sooh

single bed
cama de solteiro
KAH-mah d sohl-TAY-rooh

double bed
cama de casal
KAH-mah d kah-ZAHL

floor
andar
ahn-DAHR

front desk / reception
receção *f*
reh-seh-soan

hotel manager
diretor *m* / **diretora** *f* **do hotel**
dee-reh-TOHR / dee-reh-TOH-rah
d oh-TEHL

indoor pool
piscina coberta
peesh-SEE-nah koo-BEHR-tah

key
chave *f*
SHAH-v

kitchenette
kitchenette *f*
keet-shee-NEHT

luggage cart
carro de bagagem
KAH-rrooh d bah-GAH-jain

towels
toalhas
tooh-AH-llash

room service
serviço de quartos
sehr-VEE-sooh d KWAHR-toosh

lobby
átrio
AH-tree-ooh

wake-up call
serviço de despertar
sehr-VEE-sooh d desh-pehr-TAHR

reservation
reserva
reh-ZEHR-vah

guest
hóspede *m*
OSH-p-d

check-in	**check-in** *m*	check-in
check-out	**check-out** *m*	check-out
complimentary breakfast	**pequeno-almoço gratuito**	peh-KEH-noo ahl-MOH-sooh grah-TOOEE-tooh
king-size bed	**cama extra grande**	KAH-mah EH-shtrah GRAN-d
late charge	**taxa de pagamento atrasado**	TAH-shah d pah-gah-MEN-tooh ah-trah-ZAH-dooh
full	**cheio**	SHAY-ooh
parking pass	**passe de estacionamento** *m*	PAH-s d esh-tah-see-ooh-nah-MEN-tooh
pay-per-view movie	**filme pago por visualização** *m*	FEEL-m PAH-gooh poor vee-zooh-ah-lee-za-SOAN
queen-size bed	**cama de casal**	KAH-mah d kah-ZAHL
rate	**taxa**	TAH-shah
vacancy	**lugar vago**	loo-GAHR VAH-gooh

city-centre / downtown
centro / baixa
SEN-trooh / BAHI-shah

city
cidade *f*
see-DAH-d

metropolis
metrópole *f*
meh-TROH-poh-l

capital
capital *f*
kah-pee-TAHL

district
bairro
BAHI-rroh

region
região *f*
rreh-jee-OAN

centre
centro
SEN-trooh

industrial zone
zona industrial
ZOH-nah een-dush-tree-AHL

seaside resort
estância balnear
esh-TAHN-see-ah bahl-nee-AHR

old town
centro histórico
SEN-trooh eesh-TOH-ree-kooh

ski resort
estância de esqui
esh-TAHN-see-ah d esh-KEE

small town
vila
VEE-lah

suburb
subúrbios
sooh-BOOR-bee-oosh

village
aldeia
ahl-DAY-ah

winter resort
estância de inverno
esh-TAHN-see-ah d een-VEHR-nooh

alley
viela
vee-EH-lah

boulevard
avenida
ah-v-NEE-dah

motorway
autoestrada
aw-toh-sh-TRAH-dah

country road
estrada de terra batida
esh-TRAH-dah d TEH-rrah
bah-TEE-dah

toll road
portagem *f*
poor-TAH-jain

street
rua
ROOH-ah

bicycle lane
ciclovia
see-kloh-VEE-ah

bicycle path
ciclovia
see-kloh-VEE-ah

crossroads / intersection
cruzamento
crooh-zah-MEN-tooh

traffic lights
semáforos
seh-MAH-fooh-roosh

red light
vermelho
ver-MAH-llooh

orange light
amarelo
ah-mah-REH-looh

green light
verde
VER-d

roundabout
rotunda
rooh-TOON-dah

pedestrian crossing
passagem de peões *f*
pah-SAH-jain d pee-OINSH

pavement
passeio
pah-SAY-ooh

bridge
ponte *f*
PON-t

footbridge
ponte pedonal *f*
PON-t peh-dooh-NAHL

overpass
passagem superior *f*
pah-SAH-jain sooh-peh-REE-ohr

underpass
passagem subterrânea *f*
pah-SAH-jain soob-teh-RRAH-nee-ah

tunnel
tunel
TOOH-nel

road
estrada
esh-TRAH-dah

street corner
esquina
esh-KEE-nah

one-way street
rua de sentido único
rooah d sen-TEE-dooh OOH-nee-kooh

avenue	**avenida**	ah-v-NEE-dah
main road	**estrada principal**	esh-TRAH-dah preen-see-PAHL
side street	**estrada lateral**	esh-TRAH-dah lah-teh-RAHL
expressway	**via rápida**	VEE-ah RAH-pee-dah
four-lane road	**estrada com quatro faixas**	esh-TRAH-dah kom KWAH-trooh FAHI-shash
two-lane road	**estrada com duas faixas**	esh-TRAH-dah kom DOO-ash FAHI-shash
fast lane	**faixa de ultrapassagem**	FAHI-shah d ool-trah-pah-SAH-jain
left lane	**faixa da esquerda**	FAHI-shah dah esh-KEHR-dah
right lane	**faixa da direita**	FAHI-shah dah dee-RAY-tah
breakdown lane	**berma**	BEHR-mah

attractions
atrações *f*
ah-trah-SOINSH

casino
casino
kah-ZEE-nooh

guide book
guia
GHEE-ah

park
parque *m*
PAHR-k

guided tour
visita guiada
vee-ZEE-tah ghee-AH-dah

information
informações *f*
een-foor-mah-SOINSH

itinerary
itinerário
ee-tee-neh-RAH-ree-ooh

ruins
ruínas
roo-EE-nash

monument
monumento
mooh-nooh-MEN-tooh

museum
museu
mooh-ZEH-ooh

national park
parque nacional *m*
PAHR-k nah-see-ooh-NAHL

sightseeing
turismo
too-REESH-mooh

souvenirs
recordações f
rreh-koor-dah-SOINSH

tour bus
autocarro turístico
aw-toh-KAH-rrooh too-REESH-tee-kooh

tourist
turista
too-REE-sh-tah

entrance fee / price	**preço de entrada**	PREH-sooh d ehn-TRAH-dah
to buy a souvenir	**comprar uma recordação**	kom-PRAHR oohma rreh-koor-dah-SOAN
to do a tour	**fazer uma visita**	fah-ZEHR oohma vee-ZEE-tah
tour guide	**guia turístico**	GHEE-ah too-REESH-tee-kooh

airport
aeroporto
ah-eh-roh-POHR-tooh

bank
banco
BAHN-kooh

bus stop
paragem de autocarro _f_
pah-RAH-jain d aw-toh-KAH-rrooh

church
igreja
ee-GRAY-jah

cinema
cinema _m_
see-NEH-mah

city / town hall
câmara municipal
KAH-mah-rah mooh-nee-see-PAHL

department store
armazéns
ahr-mah-ZAINSH

factory
fábrica
FAH-bree-kah

fire station
quartel de bombeiros
KWAHR-tel d bom-BAY-roosh

hospital
hospital
osh-pee-TAHL

hotel
hotel
oh-TEHL

library
livraria
lee-vrah-REE-ah

theatre
teatro
tee-AH-trooh

museum
museu
mooh-ZEH-ooh

parking area
zona de estacionamento
ZOH-nah d esh-tah-see-ooh-nah-MEN-tooh

playground
parque infantil *m*
PAHR-k een-fan-TEEL

police station
esquadra da polícia
esh-KWAH-drah dah pooh-LEE-see-ah

post office
correios
koo-RRAY-oosh

prison
prisão *f*
pree-SOAN

restaurant
restaurante *m*
resh-taw-RAN-tee

school
escola
esh-koh-LAH

taxi stand
paragem de táxis *f*
pah-RAH-jain d TAH-ksish

harbour
porto
POHR-tooh

square
praça
PRAH-sah

supermarket
supermercado
sooh-pehr-mehr-KAH-dooh

railway station
estação de caminhos-de-ferro *f*
esh-tah-SOAN d kah-MEE-nioosh d FEH-rrooh

How do I get to the railway station?	**Qual é o caminho para a estação de caminhos-de-ferro?**	kwahl eh ooh kah-MEE-niooh PAH-rah ah esh-tah-SOAN d kah-MEE-nioosh d FEH-rrooh?
Where can I find a taxi?	**Onde posso apanhar um táxi?**	ohnd POH-sooh ah-pah-NIAHR oohm TAH-ksee?

snorkel
tubo de mergulho
TOOH-booh d mehr-GOOH-llooh

swimming goggles
óculos de natação
OH-kooh-loosh d nah-tah-SOAN

beach ball
bola de praia
BOH-lah d PRAHI-ah

hat
chapéu
shah-PEH-OOH

diving mask
máscara de mergulho
MAHSH-kah-rah d mehr-GOOH-llooh

sunglasses
óculos de sol
OH-kooh-loosh d sohl

swimming cap
touca de banho
TOH-kah d BAH-niooh

swimming costume
fato de banho
FAH-tooh d BAH-niooh

sunscreen
protetor solar
proh-teh-TOHR sooh-LAHR

beach towel
toalha de praia
tooh-AH-llah d PRAHI-ah

beach	**praia**	PRAH-ee-ah
bikini	**biquíni**	bee-KEE-nee
sun lounger	**espreguiçadeira**	esh-preh-ghee-sah-DAY-rah
to sunbathe	**tomar banhos de sol**	too-MAHR BAH-nioosh d sohl
to swim	**nadar**	nah-DAHR

 HEALTH

medicines
remédios / medicamentos
reh-MEH-dee-oosh /
meh-dee-kah-MEN-toosh

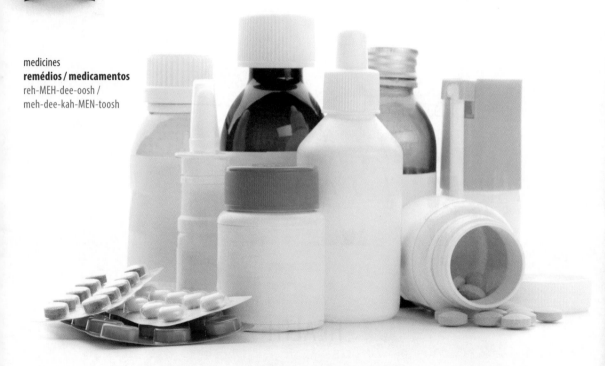

eye drops
gotas para os olhos
GOH-tash PAH-rah oosh
OH-lloosh

painkiller
analgésico
ah-nahl-JEH-zee-kooh

syrup
xarope *m*
shah-ROH-p

to take medicine
tomar remédios / medicamentos
too-MAHR reh-MEH-dee-oosh /
meh-dee-kah-MEN-toosh

shot / injection
vacina / injeção *f*
vah-SEE-nah / een-jeh-SOAN

sleeping pill
comprimido para dormir
kom-pree-MEE-dooh pah-rah
doohr-MEER

plaster
penso
PEHN-sooh

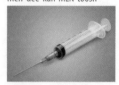

syringe
seringa
seh-REEN-gah

gauze
gaze *f*
GAH-z

pill
comprimido
kom-pree-MEE-dooh

tablet
pastilha
pash-TEE-llah

ointment
pomada
pooh-MAH-dah

hospital
hospital
osh-pee-TAHL

nurse
enfermeiro *m* **/ enfermeira** *f*
en-fehr-MAY-rooh / en-fehr-MAY-rah

doctor / physician
médico *m* **/ médica** *f*
MEH-dee-kooh / MEH-dee-kah

operation / surgery
operação / cirurgia *f*
oh-peh-rah-SOAN / see-roor-JEE-ah

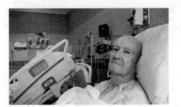

patient
paciente *m*
pah-see-EHN-t

waiting room
sala de espera
SAH-lah d esh-PEH-rah

check-up	**exame** *m*	eh-ZAH-m
diagnosis	**diagnóstico**	diahh-NOSH-tee-kooh
pharmacy / chemist's	**farmácia**	fahr-MAH-see-ah

prescription	**receita**	rre-SAY-tah
specialist	**especialista**	esh-peh-see-ah-LEESH-tah
treatment	**tratamento**	trah-tah-MEN-tooh

allergist
alergologista *m/f*
ah-lehr-gooh-looh-JEESH-tah

dentist
dentista *m/f*
den-TEESH-tah

gynecologist
ginecologista *m/f*
jee-neh-koh-loh-JEESH-tah

pediatrician
pediatra *m/f*
peh-dee-AH-trah

physiotherapist
fisioterapeuta *m/f*
fee-zee-oh-teh-rah-PEW-tah

midwife
parteira *m/f*
par-TAY-rah

ophthalmologist
oftalmologista *m/f*
of-tahl-mooh-looh-JEESH-tah

surgeon
cirurgião *m/f*
seer-oor-jee-OAN

anaesthesiologist	**anestesiologista** *m/f*	ah-nez-teh-zee-ooh-looh-JEESH-tah
cardiologist	**cardiologista** *m/f*	kahr-dee-ooh-looh-JEESH-tah
dermatologist	**dermatologista** *m/f*	dehr-mah-tooh-looh-JEESH-tah
neurologist	**neurologista** *m/f*	new-roh-loh-JEESH-tah
oncologist	**oncologista** *m/f*	ohn-koh-loh-JEESH-tah
psychiatrist	**psiquiatra** *m/f*	psee-kee-AH-trah
radiologist	**radiologista** *m/f*	rah-dee-ooh-looh-JEESH-tah

to feel good
sentir-se bem
sehn-TEER-s bain

to blow your nose
assoar o nariz
ah-sooh-AHR ooh nah-REESH

to feel sick
sentir-se mal
sen-TEER-s mahl

to catch a cold
apanhar uma constipação
ah-pah-NIAHR OOH-mah
konsh-tee-pah-SOAN

to sneeze
espirrar
esh-pee-RRAHR

to faint
desfalecer
desh-fah-I-SEHR

to have a cold
ter uma constipação
tehr OOH-mah konsh-tee-pah-SOAN

to cough
tossir
tooh-SEEHR

to pass out
desmaiar
desh-mahi-AHR

to be tired
estar cansado
esh-TAHR kahn-SAH-dooh

to be exhausted
estar exausto
esh-TAHR ee-ZAOOSH-tooh

to have back pain
ter dores de costas
tehr DOH-rsh d KOSH-tash

to have earache
ter dores de ouvido
tehr DOH-rsh d oh-VEE-dooh

to have a headache
ter uma dor de cabeça
tehr OOH-mah doh d kah-BEH-sah

to have a sore throat
ter a garganta inflamada
tehr ah gahr-GAHN-tah een-flah-MAH-dah

to have toothache
ter dor de dentes
tehr dohr d DEN-tsh

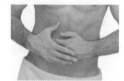

to have a stomach ache
ter dores de estômago
tehr DOH-rsh d esh-TOH-mah-gooh

to have a temperature
ter febre
tehr FEH-br

to have diarrhoea
ter diarreia
tehr dee-ah-RRAY-ah

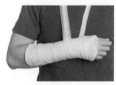

to break an arm
partir um braço
pahr-TEER oohm BRAH-sooh

to be constipated
ter prisão de ventre
tehr pree-SOAN d VEHN-tr

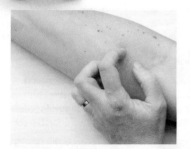

to have a rash
ter uma irritação de pele
tehr OOH-mah ee-rre-tah-SOAN d PEH-I

to be allergic to
ser alérgico a
sehr ah-LEHR-jee-kooh ah

to vomit
vomitar
vooh-mee-TAHR

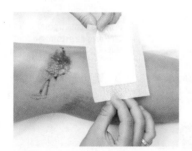

to hurt
magoar-se
mah-goo-AHR-s

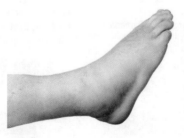

to swell
inchar
een-SHAHR

to suffer from
sofrer de
sooh-FREHR d

chicken pox
varicela
vah-ree-SEH-lah

runny nose
nariz congestionado
nah-REESH kon-jesh-tee-ooh-NAH-dooh

cough
tosse *f*
TOH-s

diarrhoea
diarreia
dee-ah-RRAY-ah

heart attack
ataque cardíaco
ah-TAH-k kahr-DEE-ah-kooh

fever
febre *f*
FEH-br

headache
dor de cabeça *f*
dohr d kah-BEH-sah

injury
lesão *f*
I-SOAN

sore throat
garganta inflamada
gahr-GAHN-tah een-flah-MAH-dah

asthma
asma
ASH-mah

flu
gripe *f*
GREE-p

health
saúde *f*
sah-OOH-d

hepatitis
hepatite *f*
eh-pah-TEE-t

heart disease
doença cardíaca
dooh-EHN-sah kahr-DEE-ah-kah

stomach ache
dor de estômago *f*
dohr d esh-TOH-mah-gooh

mouth ulcer
afta
AHF-tah

wound
ferida
feh-REE-dah

common cold	**constipação simples** *f*	konsh-tee-pah-SOAN SEEM-plesh		pain	**dor** *f*	dohr
fracture	**fratura**	frah-TOOH-rah		painful	**doloroso**	dooh-looh-ROH-sooh
illness	**doença**	dooh-EHN-sah		painless	**indolor**	een-dooh-LOHR
mumps	**papeira**	pah-PAY-rah		to be ill	**estar doente**	esh-TAHR dooh-EHN-t

emergency number
número de emergência
nooh-meh-rooh d ee-mehr-JEHN-see-ah

firefighter
bombeiro
bom-BAY-rooh

policeman
agente da polícia *m/f*
ah-JEN-t dah pooh-LEE-see-ah

fire engine
carro de bombeiros
KAH-rooh d bom-BAY-roosh

police car
carro de polícia
KAH-rooh d pooh-LEE-see-ah

ambulance
ambulância
ahm-booh-LAHN-see-ah

accident
acidente *m*
ah-see-DEHN-t

paramedics
paramédicos
pah-rah-MEH-dee-koosh

emergency
emergência
eh-mehr-JEN-see-ah

fire
incêndio
een-SEHN-dee-ooh

patient
paciente *m*
pah-see-EHNT

police
polícia
pooh-LEE-see-ah

 SPORTS

badminton racket
raquete de badmington *f*
rah-KET d badmington

ball
bola
BOH-lah

baseball
bola de baseball
BOH-lah d baseball

bicycle
bicicleta
bee-see-KLEH-tah

bowling ball
bola de bowling
BOH-lah d bowling

cap
boné *m*
boh-NEH

football
bola de futebol
BOH-lah d football

glove
luva
LOOH-vah

net
rede *f*
REH-d

goggles
óculos de proteção
OH-kooh-loosh d prooh-teh-SOAN

golf ball
bola de golfe
BOH-lah d golf

helmet
capacete *m*
kah-pah-SEH-t

goal
baliza
bah-LEE-zah

lane
pista
PEESH-tah

hockey puck
disco de hóquei
DEESH-kooh d OH-kay

hockey stick
stick de hóquei
steek d OH-kay

saddle
sela
SEH-lah

ice-skates
patins de gelo
pah-TEENS d JEH-looh

skates
patins
pah-TEENS

ski poles
bastões de esqui *m*
bash-TOINSH d esh-KEE

167

skis
esquis
esh-KEESH

snowboard
prancha de snowboard
PRAN-shah d snowboard

surfboard
prancha de surf
PRAN-shah d surf

squash racket
raquete de squash *f*
rah-KET d squash

swimming costume
fato de banho
FAH-tooh d BAH-niooh

tennis ball
bola de ténis
BOH-lah d TEH-neesh

tennis racket
raquete de ténis *f*
rah-KET d TEH-neesh

volleyball
bola de vólei
BOH-lah d VOH-lay

weights
pesos
PEH-zoosh

baseball
baseball
baseball

bowling
bowling
bowling

football
futebol
football

hiking
caminhada
kah-mee-NIAH-dah

hockey
hóquei
OH-kay

cycling
ciclismo
see-KLEESH-mooh

horseriding
equitação f
eh-kee-tah-SOAN

running
correr
kooh-RREHR

skating
patinagem
pah-tee-NAH-jain

skiing
esqui
esh-KEE

swimming
natação
nah-tah-SOAN

tennis
ténis
TEH-neesh

volleyball
vóleibol
volleyball

weightlifting
levantamento de pesos
leh-vahn-tah-MEHN-tooh d PEH-zoosh

basketball court
campo de basket
KAHM-pooh d basket

boxing ring
ringue de boxe *m*
REENG d box

golf course
campo de golf
KAHM-pooh d golf

fitnesscentre
centro de fitness
SEHN-trooh d fitness

football pitch
campo de futebol
KAHM-pooh d football

football ground
campo de futebol
KAHM-pooh d football

golf club
clube de golf *m*
kloob d golf

gym
ginásio
jee-NAH-zee-ooh

playground
parque infantil *m*
PAHR-k een-fahn-TEEL

racecourse
hipódromo
ee-POH-drooh-mooh

race track
pista de automobilismo
PEESH-tah d aw-toh-mooh-bee-
LEESH-mooh

recreation area
zona recreativa
ZOH-nah reh-kreh-ah-TEE-vah

skating rink
ringue de patinagem *m*
REENG d pah-tee-NAH-jain

sports ground
campo desportivo
KAHM-pooh desh-poohr- TEE-vooh

stadium
estádio
esh-TAH-dee-ooh

swimming pool
piscina
peesh-SEE-nah

tennis club
clube de ténis *m*
kloob d TEH-neesh

tennis court
court de ténis
KOH-rt d TEH-neesh

NATURE

landscape
paisagem *f*
pahi-ZAH-jain

bay
baía
bah-EE-ah

beach
praia
PRAHI-ah

cave
gruta
GROOH-tah

creek
riacho
ree-AH-shooh

desert
deserto
deh-ZEHR-tooh

forest	woods
floresta	**bosque**
floh-RESH-tah	BOSH-k

hill
colina
kooh-LEE-nah

earth
terra
TEH-rrah

island
ilha
EE-llah

lake
lago
LAH-gooh

mountain
montanha
mohn-TAH-niah

ocean
oceano
oh-see-AH-nooh

peak
pico
PEE-kooh

plain
planície *f*
plah-NEE-see

river
rio
REE-ooh

pond
lagoa
LAH-gooh-ah

sea
mar
mahr

stream
riacho
ree-AH-shooh

swamp
pântano
PAHN-tahn-nooh

valley
vale *m*
VAH-I

waterfall
catarata
kah-tah-RAH-tah

weather
tempo
TEHM-pooh

| What's the weather like? | **Como está o tempo?** | KOH-mooh shtah ooh TEHM-poooh? |
| What's the forecast for tomorrow? | **Qual é a previsão para amanhã?** | kwahl eh ah preh-vee-ZOAN PAH-rah ah-mah-NIAN? |

blizzard
tempestade de neve *f*
tehm-pesh-TAH-d
d NEH-v

cold
frio
FREE-ooh

drizzle
chuviscos
shoo-VEESH-koosh

flood
cheias
SHAY-ash

frost
geada
jee-AH-dah

humidity
humidade *f*
ooh-mee-DAH-d

Celsius
Celsius
SEHL-see-oosh

cyclone
ciclone *m*
see-KLOHN

dry
seco
SEH-kooh

fog
nevoeiro
neh-vooh-AY-rooh

hail
granizo
grah-NEE-zooh

hurricane
furacão *m*
fooh-rah-KOAN

cloud
nuvem *f*
NOO-vain

degree
graus
GRAH-oosh

dry season
época seca
EH-pooh-kah SEH-kah

forecast
previsão *f*
preh-vee-ZOAN

heat
calor
kah-LOHR

ice
gelo
JEH-looh

cloudy
nublado
noo-BLAH-dooh

dew
orvalho
ohr-VAH-llooh

Fahrenheit
Fahrenheit
Fah-rehn-ahit

freeze
gelar
jeh-LAHR

hot
quente
KEHN-t

lightning
relâmpago
rreh-LAHM-pah-gooh

rain
chuva
SHOO-vah

rainy season
época das chuvas
EH-pooh-kah dash
SHOO-vash

snowy
nevar
neh-VAHR

temperature
temperatura
tem-peh-rah-TOOH-rah

tsunami
tsunami
tsunami

rainstorm
temporal
tehm-pooh-RAHL

sleet
chuva de neve
SHOO-vah d NEH-v

storm
tempestade f
tem-pesh-TAH-d

thunder
trovão
troo-VOAN

typhoon
tufão
tooh-FOAN

windy
ventoso
vehn-TOH-zooh

rainbow
arco-íris
AHR-kooh EE-reesh

snow
neve f
NEH-v

sun
sol
sohl

thunderstorm
trovoada
troo-voo-AH-dah

warm
quente
KEHN-t

rainy
chuvoso
shoo-VOH-zooh

snowstorm
tempestade de neve
tem-pesh-TAH-d
d NEH-v

sunny
soalheiro
soo-ah-LLAY-rooh

tornado
tornado
tohr-NAH-dooh

wind
vento
VEHN-tooh

aquarium
aquário
ah-KWAH-ree-ooh

cage
gaiola
gay-OH-lah

pet owner
dono *m* /
dona *f* **do animal**
DOH-nooh /
DOH-nah dooh ah-nee-MAHL

canary
canário
kah-NAH-ree-ooh

bird
pássaro
PAH-sah-rooh

dog
cão *m*
koan

cat
gato
GAH-tooh

pet shop
loja de animais
LOH-jah d ah-nee-MAHISH

fish
peixe *m*
PAY-sh

gecko
geco
GEH-kooh

hamster
hamster
AHMS-tehr

guinea pig
porquinho da Índia
pohr-KEE-niooh dah
EEN-dee-ah

lizard
lagarto
lah-GAHR-tooh

rabbit
coelho
kooh-AH-llooh

rat
ratazana
rah-tah-ZAH-nah

mouse
rato
RAH-tooh

parrot
papagaio
pah-pah-GAHI-ooh

snake
cobra
KOH-brah

spider
aranha
ah-RAH-niah

cow
vaca
VAH-kah

chicken
galinha
gah-LEE-niah

donkey
burro
BOOH-rrooh

goose
ganso
GAHN-sooh

goat
cabra
KAH-brah

horse
cavalo
kah-VAH-looh

sheep
ovelha
oh-VAH-llah

duck
pato
PAH-tooh

rabbit
coelho
koo-AH-llooh

pig
porco
POHR-kooh

turkey
peru
peh-ROOH

giraffe
girafa
jee-RAH-fah

elephant
elefante *m*
ee-I-FAHN-t

jaguar
jaguar
jah-GWAHR

tiger
tigre *m*
TEE-gr

lion
leão *m*
lee-OAN

leopard
leopardo
lee-ooh-PAHR-dooh

puma
puma *m*
POOH-mah

183

hippopotamus
hipopótamo
ee-poh-POH-tah-mooh

monkey
macaco
mah-KAH-kooh

chimpanzee
chimpanzé *m*
sheem-pahn-ZEH

ostrich
avestruz *f*
ah-vesh-TROOSH

sloth
preguiça
preh-GHEE-sah

rhinoceros
rinoceronte *m*
ree-noh-sehr-
OHN-t

armadillo
tatu
TAH-tooh

iguana
iguana
ee-GHWAH-nah

kangaroo
canguru
kan-gooh-ROOH

bear
urso
OOR-sooh

zebra
zebra
ZEH-brah

hyena
hiena
ee-EH-nah

seal
foca
FOH-kah

gazelle
gazela
gah-ZEH-lah

antelope
antílope *m*
an-TEE-looh-p

python
pitão *f*
pee-TOAN

water buffalo
búfalo de água
BOO-fah-looh d
AH-goo-ah

boar
javali
jah-vah-lee

cobra
serpente *f*
sehr-PEHN-t

whale
baleia
bah-LAY-ah

killer whale
orca
OHR-kah

shark
tubarão *m*
tooh-bah-ROAN

turtle
tartaruga
tahr-tahr-OOH-gah

dolphin
golfinho
gohl-FEE-niooh

crocodile
crocodilo
krooh-kooh-DEE-looh

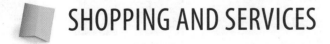

SHOPPING AND SERVICES

food market
mercado
mehr-KAH-dooh

bazaar
bazar
bah-ZAHR

bookshop
livraria
lee-vrah-REE-ah

computer shop
loja de informática
LOH-jah d een-foor-MAH-tee-kah

corner shop
loja de bairro
LOH-jah d BAHI-RROOH

farmers' market
mercado agrícola
mehr-KAH-dooh ah-GREE-kooh-lah

flea market
feira da ladra
FAY-rah dah LAH-drah

flower market
florista
flooh-REESH-tah

bakery
padaria
pah-dah-REE-ah

fruit stall
banda de fruta
BAHN-dah d FROOH-tah

market
mercado
mehr-KAH-dooh

newsagent
quiosque *m*
kee-OSH-k

shoe shop
sapataria
sah-pah-tah-REE-ah

street vendor
vendedor ambulante
ven-deh-DOOHR amb-ooh-LAHN-t

supermarket
supermercado
sooh-pehr-mehr-KAH-dooh

department store	**armazéns** *m*	ahr-mah-ZAINSH
grocery store	**mercearia**	mehr-seh-ah-REE-ah
shopping centre	**centro comercial**	SEN-trooh kooh-mehr-see-AHL

sale
saldos
SAHL-doosh

checkout / till checkout
pagar
pah-GAHR

conveyor belt
tapete rolante *m*
tah-PEH-t rooh-LAHN-t

customer
cliente *m*
klee-EHN-t

price
preço
PREH-sooh

queue
fila
FEE-lah

receipt
recibo
reh-SEE-booh

cashier
caixa
KAHI-shah

shopping bag
saco de compras
SAH-kooh d KOM-prash

shopping list
lista de compras
LEESH-tah d KOM-prash

shopping basket
cesto de compras
SESH-tooh d KOM-prash

trolley
carrinho
kah-REE-niooh

bill for	**fatura para**	fah-TOO-rah PAH-rah
Can I help you?	**Em que posso ajudá-lo?**	ain k POH-sooh ah-jooh-DAH-looh?
goods	**bens**	bainsh
shopper	**comprador *m* / compradora *f***	kom-prah-DOHR / kom-prah-DOH-rah
to cost	**custar**	koosh-TAHR
to get a great bargain	**conseguir um bom preço**	kohn-seh-GHEER oohm bohm PREH-sooh
to purchase	**comprar**	kohm-PRAHR
to queue	**ficar na fila**	fee-KAHR nah FEE-lah

coat
casaco
kah-ZAH-kooh

belt
cinto
SEEN-tooh

boots
botas
BOH-tash

hat
chapéu
shah-PEW

gloves
luvas
loo-VASH

raincoat
gabardine f
gah-bahr-DEEN

jeans
calças de ganga
KAHL-sash d GAHN-gah

pyjamas
pijama m
pee-JAH-mah

jacket
blusão m
blooh-ZOAN

shoes
sapatos
sah-PAH-toosh

jumper
casaco de malha
kah-ZAH-kooh d
MAH-llah

scarf
cachecol
kash-KOHL

underwear
roupa interior
RROH-pah een-
tehr-ree-OHR

tie
gravata
grah-VAH-tah

briefs
cuecas
KWEH-kash

sweatshirt
sweatshirt *f*
sweatshirt

shirt
camisa
kah-MEE-zah

suit
fato
FAH-tooh

t-shirt
t-shirt *f*
t-shirt

undershirt
camisola interior
kah-mee-ZOH-lah een-teh-ree-OHR

socks
meias
MAY-ash

slippers
pantufas
pahn-TOOH-fash

trousers
calças
KAHL-sash

He has a hat on.	**Ele está de chapéu.**	EHl shtah d shah-PEW
These briefs are the right size.	**Estas cuecas são do tamanho certo.**	ESH-tash KWEH-kash soan dooh tah-MAH-niooh SER-tooh
What did he have on?	**O que é que ele tinha vestido?**	ooh k eh k ehl TEE-niah vesh-TEE-dooh?
I want these boxer shorts in a size 42.	**Quero estas boxers em 42.**	kerooh ESH-tash BOKS-ers ain 42

jacket
blusão m
blooh-ZOAN

boots
botas
BOH-tash

raincoat
gabardine f
gah-bahr-DEEN

gloves
luvas
LOOH-vash

hat
chapéu
shah-PEW

jeans
calças de ganga
KAHL-sash d GAHN-gah

pyjamas
pijama m
pee-JAH-mah

coat
casaco
kah-ZAH-kooh

belt
cinto
SEEN-tooh

jumper
camisola
kah-mee-ZOH-lah

pants
cuecas
KWE-kash

scarf
cachecol
kash-KOHL

skirt
camisa
kah-MEE-zah

dress
vestido
vesh-TEE-dooh

shoes
sapatos
sah-PAH-toosh

sweatshirt
sweatshirt *f*
sweatshirt

socks
meias
MAY-ash

shirt
camisa
kah-MEE-zah

t-shirt
t-shirt f
t-shirt

stockings
meias
MAY-ash

suit
fato
FAH-tooh

underwear
roupa interior
RROH-pah een-teh-ree-OHR

trousers
calças
KAHL-sash

slacks
calças
KAHL-sash

bra
soutien
sew-tee-AIN

slippers
pantufas
pahn-TOO-fash

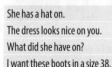

She has a hat on.	**Ela está de chapéu.**	EH-lah esh-TAH d shah-PEW
The dress looks nice on you.	**Esse vestido fica-te bem.**	EH-s vesh-TEE-dooh FEE-kah-t bain
What did she have on?	**O que é que ela tinha vestido?**	ooh k eh k EH-lah TEE-niah vesh-TEE-dooh?
I want these boots in a size 38.	**Quero estas botas em 38.**	kerooh ESH-tash BOH-tash ain 38

car repair shop
oficina de automóveis
oh-fee-SEE-nah d aw-tooh-MOH-vaysh

barber shop
barbeiro
barh-BAY-rooh

beauty salon
salão de beleza _m_
sah-LOAN d beh-LEH-zah

bicycle repair shop
oficina de bicicletas
oh-fee-SEE-nah d bee-see-KLEH-tash

watchmaker
relojoeiro
reh-looh-jooh-AY-rooh

laundromat
lavandaria self-service
lah-vahn-dah-REE-ah self-service

laundry
roupa
mehr-KAH-dooh

locksmiths
serralheiro
seh-rrah-LLAY-rooh

petrol station
bomba de gasolina
BOHM-bah d gah-zooh-LEE-nah

CULTURE AND MEDIA

blog
blogue *m*
blog

to broadcast
transmitir
transh-mee-TEER

magazine
revista
rr-VEESH-tah

newspaper
jornal
joor-NAHL

radio
rádio
RAH-dee-ooh

television
televisão *f*
t-l-vee-ZOAN

news broadcast
noticiário
nooh-tee-see-AH-ree-ooh

weather forecast
previsão do tempo
preh-vee-ZOAN dooh TEHM-pooh

blogosphere	**blogosfera**	blog-osh-FEH-rah
mass media	**meios de comunicação social**	MAY-oosh d kooh-mooh-nee-kah-SOAN sooh-see-AHL
news	**notícias**	noo-TEE-see-ash
press	**imprensa** *m*	eem-PREHN-sah
tabloid	**tablóide** *m*	tahb-LOHID
programme	**programa**	prooh-GRAH-mah
soap	**telenovela** *m*	teh-leh-nooh-VEH-lah
drama	**drama** *f*	DRAH-mah
series	**série** *m*	SEH-ree
film	**filme**	FEEL-m
documentary	**documentário** *m*	dooh-kooh-mehn-TAH-ree-ooh
music programme	**programa musical** *m*	prooh-GRAH-mah mooh-zee-KAHL
sports programme	**programa desportivo** *m*	prooh-GRAH-mah desh-poor-TEE-vooh
talk show	**programa de entrevistas**	prooh-GRAH-mah d en-treh-VEESH-tash
episode	**episódio**	eh-pee-ZOH-dee-ooh
business news	**notícias de economia**	noo-TEE-see-ash d ee-koh-noh-MEE-ah
sports report	**informação desportiva**	een-foor-mah-SOAN desh-poor-tee-vah
book review	**crítica literária**	KREE-tee-kah leet-RAH-ree-ah
ad / advertisement	**anúncio**	ah-NOON-see-ooh

message
mensagem *f*
mehn-SAH-jain

address / URL
endereço
ehnd-REH-sooh

application / app
aplicação *f*
ah-plee-kah-SOAN

network
canal
kah-NAHL

inbox	**caixa de entrada**	KAHI-shah d ehn-TRAH-dah
IP address	**endereço IP** *f*	ehnd-REH-sooh IP
internet	**Internet**	een-tehr-NEHT
website	**página Web**	PAH-jee-nah web
mail	**correio**	kooh-RRAY-ooh
search engine	**motor de busca**	mooh-TOHR d BOOSH-kah
to search	**pesquisar**	pesh-kee-ZAHR
to share	**partilhar**	pahr-tee-LLAHR
to log in	**entrar**	ehn-TRAHR

to send
enviar
ehn-vee-AHR

login
nome de utilizador *m*
NOH-m d ooh-tee-lee-zah-DOHR

to log out
sair
sah-EER

to upload	**enviar**	ehn-vee-AHR
to download	**descarregar**	desh-kah-rregh-AHR
to tag	**etiquetar**	eh-teek-TAHR
to comment	**comentar**	koh-mehn-TAHR
to publish	**publicar**	pooh-blee-KAHR
to contact	**contactar**	kont-takt-AHR
to receive	**receber**	reh-seh-BEHR
to add	**adicionar**	ah-dee-see-ooh-NAHR

link
ligação *f*
lee-gah-SOAN

CD
CD *m*
CD

CD-ROM
CD-ROM *m*
CD-ROM

DVD
DVD *m*
DVD

mouse
rato
RRAH-tooh

keyboard
teclado
teh-KLAH-dooh

USB flash drive
memória USB
meh-MOH-ree-ah USB

laptop
portátil
poor-TAH-teel

modem
modem
MOH-dehm

monitor
monitor
mooh-nee-TOHR

router
router
RROOH-tehr

tablet
tablet
TAH-blet

printer
impressora
eem-preh-SOH-rah

scanner
scaner
scanner

to copy	**copiar**	kooh-pee-AHR	to print	**imprimir**	eem-pree-MEEHR
to delete	**apagar**	ah-pah-GAHR	to save	**guardar**	gwhar-DAHR
desktop	**ambiente de trabalho**	ahm-bee-EHNT d trah-BAH-llooh	to scan	**digitalizar**	dee-gee-tah-lee-ZAHR
			screenshot	**captura de ecrã**	kap-TOOH-rah d eh-KRAN
file	**ficheiro**	fee-SHAY-rooh	server	**servidor**	sehr-vee-DOHR
folder	**pasta**	PASH-tah	software	**software**	software
offline	**offline**	offline	to undo	**voltar atrás**	vohl-TAHR ah-TRASH
online	**online**	online	virus	**vírus**	VEE-roosh
password	**senha**	SAH-niah			

at
arroba
ah-RROH-bah

hash
cardinal
kar-dee-NAHL

percent
percentagem *f*
per-sen-TAH-jain

circumflex
acento circunflexo
ah-SEN-tooh seer-
koon-FLEX-ooh

ampersand
símbolo de *e*
SEEM-booh-looh d eh

asterisk
asterisco
asht-REESH-
kooh

tilde
til
teel

tab key
tecla tab
TEH-klah tab

caps lock key
tecla caps lock
TEK-klah caps lock

shift key
tecla shift
TEH-klah shift

ctrl (control) key
tecla control
TEH-klah control

exclamation mark
ponto de exclamação
PON-tooh d esh-klah-
mah-SOAN

alt (alternate) key
tecla alt
TEH-klah alt

spacebar key
barra de espaço
BAH-rrah d esh-PAH-sooh

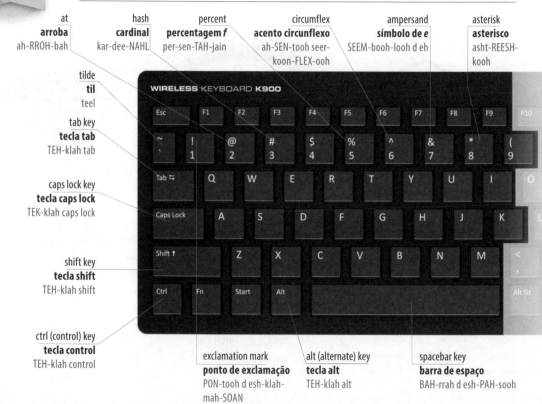

minus / dash
hífen / travessão *m*
EE-fehn / trahv-SOAN

plus
mais
MAHISH

equal
igual
eeh-gwahl

colon
dois pontos
doish PON-toosh

semicolon
ponto e vírgula
POHN-tooh ee VEER-gooh-lah

dot / full stop
ponto final
POHN-tooh fee-nahl

question mark
ponto de interrogação
PON-tooh d een-teh-rrooh-gah-SOAN

enter key
tecla enter
TEH-klah enter

forward slash
barra para a frente
BAH-rrah PAH-rah ah FREHN-t

back slash
barra para trás
BAH-rrah PAH-rah trash

backspace key
tecla de apagar
TEH-klah d ah-pah-GAHR

delete or del key
tecla delete ou del
TEH-klah delete aw del

amusement park
parque de diversões *m*
PAHR-k d dee-vehr-SOINSH

aquarium
aquário
ah-KWAH-ree-ooh

art gallery
galeria de arte
gah-leh-REE-ah d AHR-t

art museum
museu de arte
mooh-ZEW d AHR-t

botanical garden
jardim botânico
jahr-DEEM booh-TAH-nee-kooh

cinema
cinema *m*
see-NEH-mah

circus
circo
SEER-kooh

discotheque
discoteca
deesh-kooh-TEH-kah

garden
jardim
jahr-DEEM

night club
clube noturno *m*
kloob noh-TOOR-nooh

trade fair / trade show
feira
FAY-rah

opera house
ópera
OH-peh-rah

concert hall
sala de concertos
SAH-lah d kohn-SEHR-toosh

park
parque *m*
PAHR-k

planetarium
planetário
plah-neh-TAH-ree-ooh

science museum
museu de ciência
mooh-ZEW d see-EHN-see-ah

sights
vistas
VEESH-tash

theatre
teatro
tee-AH-trooh

tourist attraction
atração turística *f*
ah-trah-SOAN tooh-REESH-tee-kah

water park
parque aquático *m*
PAHR-k ah-KWAH-tee-kooh

zoo
jardim zoológico
jahr-DEEM zooh-LOH-jee-kooh

accordion
acordeão *m*
ah-kohr-dee-OAN

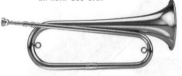

bugle
corneta
kohr-NEH-tah

clarinet
clarinete *m*
klah-ree-NEH-t

bagpipes
gaita de foles
GAHI-tah d FOH-lsh

castanets
castanholas
kash-tah-NIOH-lash

banjo
banjo
BAHN-jooh

cymbals
pratos
PRAH-toosh

cello
violoncelo
veew-lohn-SEH-looh

drum
tambor
tahm-BOHR

electric guitar
guitarra elétrica
ghee-TAH-rrah ee-LEH-tree-kah

flute
flauta
FLAW-tah

drum set
bateria
bah-teh-REE-ah

harmonica
gaita de beiços
GAHI-tah d BAY-soosh

guitar
viola
vee-OH-lah

grand piano
piano de cauda
pee-AH-nooh d KAW-dah

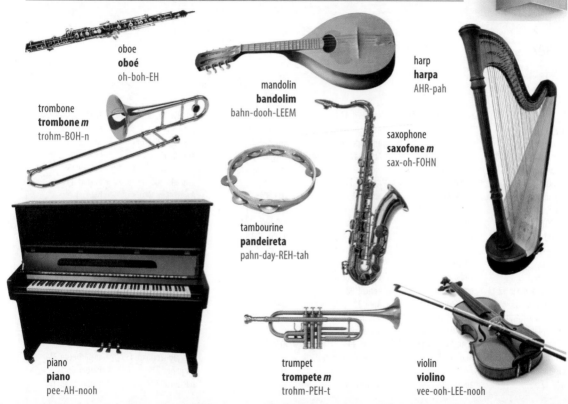

oboe
oboé
oh-boh-EH

mandolin
bandolim
bahn-dooh-LEEM

harp
harpa
AHR-pah

trombone
trombone *m*
trohm-BOH-n

saxophone
saxofone *m*
sax-oh-FOHN

tambourine
pandeireta
pahn-day-REH-tah

piano
piano
pee-AH-nooh

trumpet
trompete *m*
trohm-PEH-t

violin
violino
vee-ooh-LEE-nooh

Index